The Best Sight Word Book Ever!

Learn 170 High-Frequency Words and Increase Fluency and Comprehension Skills

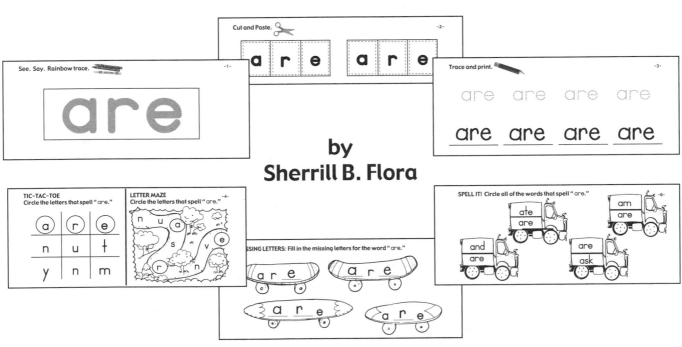

by
Sherrill B. Flora

Illustrated by
Timothy M. Irwin

Publisher
Key Education
Publishing Company, LLC
Minneapolis, Minnesota

CONGRATULATIONS ON YOUR PURCHASE OF A KEY EDUCATION PRODUCT!

The editors at Key Education are former teachers who bring experience, enthusiasm, and quality to each and every product. Thousands of teachers have looked to the staff at Key Education for new and innovative resources to make their work more enjoyable and rewarding. Key Education is committed to developing and publishing educational materials that will assist teachers in building a strong and developmentally appropriate curriculum for young children.

PLAN FOR GREAT TEACHING EXPERIENCES WHEN YOU USE
EDUCATIONAL MATERIALS FROM KEY EDUCATION PUBLISHING COMPANY, LLC

Credits
Author: Sherrill B. Flora
Creative Director: Annette Hollister-Papp
Inside Illustrations: Timothy M. Irwin
Cover Design: Mary Eden
Editors: George C. Flora and Karen Seberg
Production: Key Education Staff

Key Education welcomes manuscripts and product ideas from teachers.
For a copy of our submission guidelines, please send a self-addressed, stamped envelope to:

Key Education Publishing Company, LLC
Acquisitions Department
9601 Newton Avenue South
Minneapolis, Minnesota 55431

Standard Book Number: 978-1-933052-67-0
The Best Sight Word Book Ever!
Copyright © 2007 by Key Education Publishing Company, LLC
Minneapolis, Minnesota 55431

Contents

Introduction

What are sight words and why are they so important? Sight words are considered to be those words that occur frequently in our written language. There are over 600,000 words in the English language — 15 of these words comprise 25 percent of all written material and 100 of these words comprise 50 percent of all written and spoken material. To become a functional reader, students must be able to instantly identify these words.

Current reading research has shown that students who have automatic word identification skills also have good comprehension skills and are able to read fluently. Children who struggle with sight word recognition also struggle with comprehension and fluency. Struggling readers will often have to reread text in order to gain meaning and are forced to spend far too much time decoding unknown words.

The Best Sight Word Book Ever! provides a wealth of materials: teaching suggestions, activity ideas, multi-sensory experiences, word wall activities, a reproducible chart for organizing sight word lists, a checklist for documenting student progress, and a reproducible multi-sensory 6-page sight word activity booklet for each of the 170 words presented. Everything a teacher needs to teach and help students develop strong sight word identification skills.

The 170 words in *The Best Sight Word Book Ever!* were researched and compiled from the following lists:
- Dolch Sight Word List *(Pre-primer, Primer, Grades 1 and 2)*
- The 100 Most Frequent Words in Books for Beginning Readers
- The Word Bank of High Frequency Writing Words
- Dr. Fry's Instant Words
- American Heritage Word Frequency Book
- A Basic Vocabulary of Elementary School Children

How to Effectively Use the Six-Page Sight Word Booklets

Activity directions are kept to a minimum on the sight word booklet pages. Young and struggling readers are often distracted when there is too much type on a page. The teacher should use the information provided below and on page 6 for more detailed directions for the activities found in the sight word booklets.

Page 1: See. Say. Rainbow trace. The first page of every booklet begins with a rainbow writing exercise. This is the page that introduces the new sight word. Have the children look at the word. Say the word out loud several times — in a couple of funny voices. Have the children close their eyes and say the word again and then spell the word out loud. The children should then trace the word several times, each time using a different colored crayon.

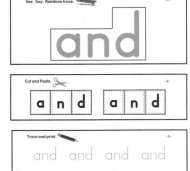

Page 2: Cut and Paste. The second page of every booklet asks the children to spell the word correctly by cutting out all of the letters and then pasting them in the correct order.

Page 3: Trace and Print. The third page of every booklet asks the children to first trace and then print the word several times.

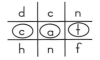

Pages 4, 5, and 6. There are 14 different types of activities and games that appear on pages 4, 5, and 6 of the student booklets. You will find the specific directions for those 14 activities listed below:

1. Tic-Tac-Toe: Tic-Tac-Toe is only used for three-letter words. The children find and circle the letters that spell the word. The word could appear horizontally, diagonally, or vertically.

2. Word Tic-Tac-Toe: Word Tic-Tac-Toe is used for those words that have either more or less than three letters. The children find and circle the designated word. The word could appear horizontally, diagonally, or vertically.

3. Letter Maze: The children will find an object or a path filled with letters. The children should circle all the letters that would correctly spell the specific word for that booklet.

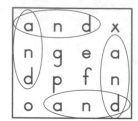

4. Word Maze: The children will find a picture filled with words. The children should circle all the words that correctly spell the specific word from that sight word booklet.

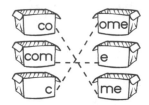

5. Word Search: The children search for the specific word from that booklet. They circle the letters that correctly spell that word. The letters could be arranged horizontally, diagonally, or vertically.

6. Pyramid Words: The first letter goes on the top line. The first and second letters go on the second line. The first, second, and third letters go on the third line and so on.

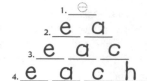

1.

2. e a

3. e a c

4. e a c h

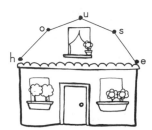

7. Blend the Word: Have the children look at the letters and then match the left side letters to the right side letters to correctly spell the word. See example.

8. Letter Connect: The children will see objects. In each object will be a letter from that booklet's featured word. The children are to draw lines to connect the letters so that the word is spelled properly.

9. Dot-To-Dot: The children are to finish the picture by connecting the dots. Instead of connecting the dots numerically, the children will connect the dots by spelling the booklet's featured word correctly.

10. Scrambled Words: The booklets featured word is all mixed up. The children look at the scrambled words and then rearrange the letters so that the word is spelled correctly.

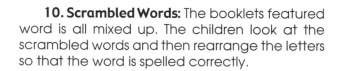

11. Missing Letters: The booklet's featured word is missing some letters. The children write in the letters that are missing.

12. Spell It!: The booklet's featured word is placed within a scene along with many other words. The children should look and then circle the featured words.

13. Coloring Words: The booklet's featured word appears in a picture or in objects within a picture. The children must look at all the words and then color the objects or sections of the picture where the featured word appears.

14. Finish The Sentence: The booklet's featured word is missing from several sentences. Have the children fill in the blanks properly and then read the sentence.

1. Go and _____ for the cat.

2. I can _____ for the book.

3. Did you _____ for the dog?

How to Introduce and Teach Sight Words

The Importance of Sight Words: Sight words or high-frequency words are seen and heard everywhere! Children must be able to identify these words instantly in order to become functional and fluent readers. The following literacy skills will increase when children are able to read sight words quickly.

- The children will be able to focus on comprehending the meaning of what they are reading rather than concentrating on decoding unknown words.
- The children will be able to use context clues more effectively.
- The children will be able to read more material.
- The children will read with greater fluency.
- Most importantly, children who have developed good sight word skills now enjoy reading!

Know Where to Start: Assessing a child's pre-existing sight word knowledge can assist a teacher or parent in knowing which words need to be taught and in choosing appropriately leveled reading material so that the child will experience success. Use the **"Sight Word Checklist for Documenting Student Progress"** found on page 9 to maintain a record of the words mastered by each child.

The guide below will give you an idea of where to begin in selecting reading materials:

> Knowledge of 0–75 words is generally considered a Pre-Kindergarten Reading Level.
> Knowledge of 76–120 words is generally considered a Kindergarten Reading Level.
> Knowledge of 121–170 words is generally considered a First Grade Reading Level.
> Knowledge of 171–210 words is generally considered a Second Grade Reading Level.
> Knowledge of 211+ words is generally considered a Third Grade Reading Level.

Understanding and Recognizing Similarities and Differences: There are a multitude of sight words that have similarities, such as was/saw, came/come, went/want, to/too, and no/on, to only name a few. There are also various numbers and alphabet letters that are easily confused, reversed, or inverted — for example, 9/6, 8/S, S/Z, p/q, d/b, m/w, n/u, c/e/o/a/, and f/t. Children must be able to visually discriminate similarities and differences in order to identify letters and eventually read words.

Before introducing sight words, the teacher needs to assess if the children understand the concepts of "same" and "different." To do this, present the children with concrete objects and make some comparisons. For example, show the children two balls— a red ball and a blue ball. Explain that they are the "same" because each one is a ball, and that they are "different" because one is red and one is blue. Continue to use objects as examples until you see that the children have a firm grasp on "same" and "different" with concrete objects. Then show the children plastic alphabet letters or alphabet wooden blocks. Present two letters at a time. Sometimes display two letters that are the "same" and sometimes display two letters that are "different." When you see that the children are able to consistently identify when the two letters are the "same" or when they are "different," then move to introducing three letters at a time (*two letters being the same and one being different*). Keep increasing the difficulty level.

Finally, challenge the children with the following paper and pencil activity. Alternate between asking the children to circle the one that is "different" or circle the ones that are the "same." The following are some suggestions that can be used for this paper and pencil activity. Make three the same and one different: m/w/m/m, o/o/a/o. b/b/b/d, q/p/q/q/, z/z/s/z, 3/8/3/3, u/u/u/n, t/t/f/t, e/e/c/e, F/E/E/E, R/R/R/P, K/R/K/K/, g/g/q/g, was/saw/saw/saw, does/does/goes/does, on/on/on/no, pot/pot/top/pot, it/it/it/if, man/men/man/man. Create activities of your own.

Important Steps for
Introducing New Sight Words

1. Carefully choose the words to be introduced: The **"Reproducible Chart for Organizing Sight Words Lists"** (found on page 10) is provided to help teachers organize their own word lists. Grade level expectations, reading programs, and the word lists already required by individual schools or school systems can vary greatly. The words in this book are organized alphabetically—allowing teachers the flexibility of choosing their own words, creating their own word lists, and deciding the order that words will be introduced to the students. The sight word lists can be individualized for whole classrooms or for each student.

2. After you have chosen a word, give each child a copy of page 1 (See. Say. Rainbow trace.) of the Sight Word Booklet:

- Ask the children to look at the word on the paper. Ask if anyone knows the word.
- Tell the children what the word is. Say the word together.
- Look at the word and say it together again.
- Say the word in a variety of fun and different ways: loud, soft, create a chant, use a silly voice, etc.
- Make a large copy of the word and add it to the classroom word wall. *(Reproducible words for the word wall can be found on pages 359–382.)*
- Spell the word out loud several times.
- Have the children complete the rainbow writing activity on page 1.
- When the children have finished rainbow writing, have them turn the paper over and spell the word from memory.

3. Extra tips and fun ideas for when a new word is first introduced:
- Ask the children to close their eyes and pretend to see the word on a television screen. Can they visualize the word? Did they see it?
- Give each child a piece of paper and ask them to write down the word from memory.
- Plan some multi-sensory activities to help increase the children's visual memory of the word. A variety of multi-sensory activities can be found on 11.

4. Continue with pages 2 (Cut and Paste.) and 3 (Trace and Print.) of the sight word booklet:
- Have the children complete these activities. Over the next several days the children can complete pages 4, 5, and 6 of the sight word booklet.
- Also plan some of the spelling (page 12), reading (pages 13–14), sentence building (pages 15–16), and reading in context activities (page 17) to provide additional experiences with the word.

5. Review, review, review, and incorporate word wall activities:
- Provide daily review of all the words that have been introduced. Use word wall activities (page 18) and continue to provide additional reading experiences that will reinforce word recognition, fluency, and comprehension.

Name _____

Directions:
- Color the first box when the word is introduced.
- Color the second box when the word is known "some" of the time.
- Color the third box when the word is mastered and place a date next to the word.

Sight Word Checklist for Documenting Student Progress

☐☐☐ a	☐☐☐ do	☐☐☐ if	☐☐☐ people	☐☐☐ this
☐☐☐ about	☐☐☐ dog	☐☐☐ in	☐☐☐ play	☐☐☐ three
☐☐☐ after	☐☐☐ down	☐☐☐ into	☐☐☐ please	☐☐☐ time
☐☐☐ again	☐☐☐ each	☐☐☐ is	☐☐☐ pretty	☐☐☐ to
☐☐☐ all	☐☐☐ eat	☐☐☐ it	☐☐☐ purple	☐☐☐ too
☐☐☐ am	☐☐☐ eight	☐☐☐ its	☐☐☐ put	☐☐☐ tree
☐☐☐ an	☐☐☐ every	☐☐☐ jump	☐☐☐ ran	☐☐☐ two
☐☐☐ and	☐☐☐ find	☐☐☐ just	☐☐☐ red	☐☐☐ under
☐☐☐ any	☐☐☐ first	☐☐☐ let	☐☐☐ ride	☐☐☐ up
☐☐☐ are	☐☐☐ five	☐☐☐ like	☐☐☐ run	☐☐☐ us
☐☐☐ as	☐☐☐ fly	☐☐☐ little	☐☐☐ said	☐☐☐ use
☐☐☐ ask	☐☐☐ for	☐☐☐ long	☐☐☐ saw	☐☐☐ very
☐☐☐ at	☐☐☐ four	☐☐☐ look	☐☐☐ say	☐☐☐ walk
☐☐☐ ate	☐☐☐ from	☐☐☐ made	☐☐☐ school	☐☐☐ want
☐☐☐ away	☐☐☐ funny	☐☐☐ make	☐☐☐ see	☐☐☐ *was*
☐☐☐ ball	☐☐☐ get	☐☐☐ many	☐☐☐ seven	☐☐☐ water
☐☐☐ be	☐☐☐ girl	☐☐☐ may	☐☐☐ she	☐☐☐ we
☐☐☐ been	☐☐☐ give	☐☐☐ me	☐☐☐ six	☐☐☐ well
☐☐☐ big	☐☐☐ go	☐☐☐ mom	☐☐☐ so	☐☐☐ went
☐☐☐ black	☐☐☐ good	☐☐☐ must	☐☐☐ some	☐☐☐ were
☐☐☐ blue	☐☐☐ got	☐☐☐ my	☐☐☐ soon	☐☐☐ what
☐☐☐ boy	☐☐☐ green	☐☐☐ new	☐☐☐ stop	☐☐☐ when
☐☐☐ brown	☐☐☐ had	☐☐☐ nine	☐☐☐ take	☐☐☐ where
☐☐☐ but	☐☐☐ has	☐☐☐ no	☐☐☐ ten	☐☐☐ which
☐☐☐ by	☐☐☐ have	☐☐☐ not	☐☐☐ than	☐☐☐ white
☐☐☐ call	☐☐☐ he	☐☐☐ now	☐☐☐ thank	☐☐☐ who
☐☐☐ came	☐☐☐ help	☐☐☐ of	☐☐☐ that	☐☐☐ will
☐☐☐ can	☐☐☐ her	☐☐☐ on	☐☐☐ the	☐☐☐ with
☐☐☐ cat	☐☐☐ here	☐☐☐ one	☐☐☐ their	☐☐☐ work
☐☐☐ come	☐☐☐ him	☐☐☐ or	☐☐☐ them	☐☐☐ would
☐☐☐ could	☐☐☐ his	☐☐☐ orange	☐☐☐ then	☐☐☐ yellow
☐☐☐ dad	☐☐☐ house	☐☐☐ our	☐☐☐ there	☐☐☐ yes
☐☐☐ day	☐☐☐ how	☐☐☐ out	☐☐☐ these	☐☐☐ you
☐☐☐ did	☐☐☐ I	☐☐☐ over	☐☐☐ they	☐☐☐ your

Reproducible Chart for Organizing Sight Word Lists

List _____	List _____	List _____	List _____	List _____
1. _____	1. _____	1. _____	1. _____	1. _____
2. _____	2. _____	2. _____	2. _____	2. _____
3. _____	3. _____	3. _____	3. _____	3. _____
4. _____	4. _____	4. _____	4. _____	4. _____
5. _____	5. _____	5. _____	5. _____	5. _____

List _____	List _____	List _____	List _____	List _____
1. _____	1. _____	1. _____	1. _____	1. _____
2. _____	2. _____	2. _____	2. _____	2. _____
3. _____	3. _____	3. _____	3. _____	3. _____
4. _____	4. _____	4. _____	4. _____	4. _____
5. _____	5. _____	5. _____	5. _____	5. _____

List _____	List _____	List _____	List _____	List _____
1. _____	1. _____	1. _____	1. _____	1. _____
2. _____	2. _____	2. _____	2. _____	2. _____
3. _____	3. _____	3. _____	3. _____	3. _____
4. _____	4. _____	4. _____	4. _____	4. _____
5. _____	5. _____	5. _____	5. _____	5. _____

List _____	List _____	List _____	List _____	List _____
1. _____	1. _____	1. _____	1. _____	1. _____
2. _____	2. _____	2. _____	2. _____	2. _____
3. _____	3. _____	3. _____	3. _____	3. _____
4. _____	4. _____	4. _____	4. _____	4. _____
5. _____	5. _____	5. _____	5. _____	5. _____

Multisensory Experiences to Build Visual Memory Skills

1. Tactile Writing (auditory, visual, tactile, & kinesthetic):

Learning to read sight words, especially high-frequency, phonetically irregular words, often means that children will simply have to memorize the word. Some children find memorizing words easy while many other children find visual memory tasks extremely difficult. Activities that utilize the auditory, visual, tactile, and kinesthetic senses can help struggling readers imprint these words and increase their ability to recall these words. The following are some recommended multi-sensory activities that can be very effective:

Cookie Sheets and Dry Materials: Tactile experiences allow children to "feel" shapes, letters, and numbers as they draw with their fingers. Fill a cookie sheet with any of the following materials: rice, clean sand, salt, glitter, coffee, sugar, seeds, small beads, or oatmeal. Let the children draw and trace with their fingers. Have them trace the word, spell each letter out loud, and then say the word.

Self-Sealing Bags and "Gooey" Materials: Fill self-sealing plastic bags with either shaving cream, liquid tempera paint, whipped cream, or jello. As you are sealing the bag, make sure that the bag is not filled with a lot of air. Then tape the top of the bag to ensure that the seal will not open. Have the children practice writing their new words by pressing down on the plastic. The letters will appear and can then be "squished" away.

Wet Writing: Have the children practice their new words by writing them on a chalkboard using a paintbrush and a small bowl of water.

Fabric Writing Boards: Older children who are uncomfortable (or think they are too old to play with sand or paint) can practice tracing their words on a board covered with a textured fabric, such as burlap, velvet, dotted swiss, or suede. Another idea is to simply glue paper to a board or to a piece of heavy card board.

2. Writing in the Air (auditory, visual, & kinesthetic):

This is an effective technique for reviewing words with your students. Use a chant or rhythm as you spell the word. Have the children practice the chant. Then ask the children to close their eyes, hold their hand that they write with up in the air, and pretend to write each letter as they spell the word. Encourage the children to use large movements—the whole arm should move.

3. Visualize The Words (auditory & visual):

Have the children pretend that they are holding a camera. They should pretend to take a picture of the word and store it inside their heads. Have them close their eyes and try to recall the picture of the word. Can they see it with their eyes closed? Have the children spell the word out loud using quiet voices. Say it louder and louder each time the word is spelled.

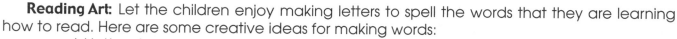

Sight Word Activities for Spelling

Spelling is not always an exciting activity for young children. Here are some ideas that will turn the boredom of spelling into fun games and activities:

Hopscotch Spelling: Draw a hopscotch grid with chalk outside on the playground, or use tape on the classroom floor, or draw one using a permanent marker and a vinyl shower curtain or tablecloth. Choose a word, and write the whole word in the top box and the letters in the boxes below. Ask the children to name each letter they land on as they "hop" and then shout the word when they reach the top box.

Put Together and Take Apart Words: Provide each child with plastic letters, alphabet cards, alphabet blocks, letter tiles, or magnetic letters. Show the children a flash card of a word. Have the children read the word out loud. Hide the flash card and then ask the children to use their alphabet letters to recreate the word. Did everyone spell it correctly?

Reading Art: Let the children enjoy making letters to spell the words that they are learning how to read. Here are some creative ideas for making words:
- mold letters from play dough
- stamp words using rubber letter stamps
- color words using stencils
- arrange letters using Wikki Sticks®
- cut and paste letters from a magazine or newspaper
- practice by using colored chalk on black construction paper

Big Group Tic-Tac-Toe: Divide the class into two groups—one group will be the "X's" and the other group will be the "O's." The teacher should draw a large tic-tac-toe grid on the chalkboard, a wipe-off board, or on chart paper. Before either of the groups can write an "X" or an "O" on the grid, the group must first spell one of their newly learned words correctly. Make sure that every child has a turn to spell a word.

Wheel of Fortune: The teacher should prepare large alphabet letter cards by printing letters on 8.5" x 11" card stock. The teacher then chooses a word and gives the letters of that word to selected students. The students stand in a line, in a mixed-up order, hiding the letters from the rest of the class. The teacher asks the class to begin guessing letters. If a letter from the hidden word is guessed, that child turns their card around so everyone can see the letter. The children should try and guess what the word is going to be.

Sight Word Activities for Reading

Here are some activities that will become classroom favorites and will make the memorization process of learning sight words much more fun!

Partner Race: The children first choose partners. *(Although they do not know that they are going to compete against their partner.)* All the children stand side by side at the back of the room. The teacher writes a word on the board, or shows the children a word on a flash card. The first partner to read the word gets to take two steps forward. The first child to reach the front of the room gets to take the teacher's spot and write or hold the word cards.

Chalkboard Race: The teacher writes two lists of words on the chalkboard. Both lists have the same words but in a different order. The children are divided into two groups and stand in two lines. The first two children in line come forward. They each read the top word on the list that is directly in front of them. If they read the word correctly, they get to erase the word and go to the back of the line. If the child does not read the word correctly, the word stays on the board and the child goes to the back of the line. The team that erases all of their words first is the winner.

Bean Bag Toss Words: The teacher creates a sight word mat from an old vinyl tablecloth or shower curtain. Using a permanent marker, draw 16 squares and write a word in each square. The children take turns tossing a bean bag. When the bean bag lands on a square, the child must read that word.

Magic Tricks: This game is similar to the old game where the bean is hidden under a cup. The teacher chooses three to five word cards and sets them up along the edge of the chalkboard or places them in a pocket chart. As a group, the children read the words. The teacher asks the children to close their eyes and then hides a small object behind one of the cards. The children must read the words again to ask where the object is hidden.

Reading Basketball: If possible, purchase a small basketball and hoop that can be put on a classroom wall. If this is not possible, you can use a waste paper basket and a small ball. Show the children, one at a time, a word card. If the child reads the word correctly, he gets to toss the ball into the basket. If not, the next child gets a turn.

Memory Match: Make two sets of word cards. Place both sets of cards facedown on a table. Have the children take turns turning over two cards at a time. They should read each card. If the cards have the same word, the child gets to keep those cards. If the words are different they must be turned back over on the table. The child with the most cards at the end of the game is the winner.

Family Feud Race: Divide the children into two groups. Just like the TV show—one child from each team comes up to the podium. On the podium is a stack of word cards and two bells. The teacher, or moderator, turns over a card and the first child to ring the bell gets to try reading the word card. If the child reads the word correctly, that team gets a point. If the child does not read the word correctly, the other child gets to try to read the word. The team with the most points after ten word cards is the winner and then gets to go to the lightening round. The lightening round provides the winning team an opportunity to earn more points. One child from the winning team is chosen to play this round. The child is given 30 seconds to read as many words as they can from the word card pile. Award one point for each word correctly read.

Swat the Word: Divide the children into two teams. On the chalkboard, or on chart paper, write two identical lists of words. Have the children stand in two lines. The first child in each line holds a fly swatter. The teacher reads a word and then the first two children run up to the board, swat that word, run back to the line, hand off the fly swatter to the next child in line, and then goes to the back of the line and sits down. The first team with everyone sitting down is the winner.

Alphabetical Word Order: Hand different word cards to four or five children. The children must work as a team to alphabetize the word cards. Once they have decided on the alphabetical sequence, the children should stand in line and hold their cards in that order. The rest of the class then reads the words and decides if the children holding the cards are correct.

| all | cat | come | down | from |

More Alphabetical Fun: Give each child two word cards and then have them find a partner. Once all of the children have found partners, have them they combine their cards (*which now totals four*) and work together to read the cards and then organize them in alphabetical order.

Organizing Groups of Words: Divide the class into groups of four. Provide each group with an identical set of word cards. Assign each group a different task. For example, one group finds all the words that begin with "T." Another group might find all the words that have an "a." When all the groups have finished their assignments, have them present the words to the rest of the class. Each group should explain what they were looking for and then read the words they thought fit into that category.

 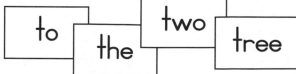

Commercially Made Games: There are also many commercially made games that are excellent for helping young children learn how to read. Here are a few of the games that your students might enjoy: Sight Word Bingo, Scrabble, Boggle, Word Searches, and Lotto.

Sight Word Activities for Sentence Building

Making Human Sentences: The teacher will need to prepare word cards and then organize them into four and five word sentences. Place the children into sentence groups. Hand them the cards in random order. The children are to look at the word cards and then arrange them into a sentence. Have each child hold a card in the proper order of the sentence.

Large Sentence Strips: Write sentences on sentence strips that can be placed in a pocket chart. Have the children read the sentence together. Point to each word as it is read. Ask the children to cover their eyes and then cover one of the words. When the children open their eyes they should tell you what word is missing. Try this same activity again, but this time try covering two of the words.

Make Up Your Own Sentences: Give each child a word card. Go around the room and have the children read the word to the class and then use the word in a sentence. When the child has finished, ask if anyone else can think of another sentence using that word. To make this game even more complicated, hand each child two word cards and have them come up with a sentence that uses both words.

Chart Paper Poems: The teacher should write a simple poem on a piece of chart paper. Using predictable text from a well-known children's story will also work. For example: "One fish, two fish, red fish, blue fish." First, have the children read the poem or text together. Next, turn off the lights and point to certain words using a flashlight. When the light flashes on a word, the children should read the word in a loud voice.

Cut-Up Sentences: The teacher should choose a short paragraph or a page from a favorite story. Write each sentence in a different color. Cut apart the sentences and give each sentence to a small group of children. The children must work together as a team to put their sentence back together. Once all the groups have completed their sentences they should read them out loud and then decide, as a class, how to organize the sentences back into the correct order. This is a difficult activity that requires the children to have a good understanding of the story and be able to fluently read the sentences. You can also discuss the main idea of the paragraph, story details, the punctuation, and the beginning and ending sentences.

Sight Word Phrases and Sentences: Children learn to read words faster when they use them in context. As soon as the children are able to read a few words, combine them into phrases or small sentences. Have the children write the phrase and then draw an illustration to go with it.

The following is a list of phrases using the sight words that appear in this book. Use these phrases as a springboard to help you write sentence strips for the children to read.

a big house	has found	let me help	under there
a big ride	has made	like this	up and down
a good jump	has run away	look at her	up here
a little one	have some	look at him	up there
about him	he had to	look at me	was made
about it	he is	look out there	we are
all day	he is funny	made a big	we eat
as he did	he said no	must be	we go out
as he said	he was	must go	we were
as I do	he would do	my cat	went away
as I said	he would try	my dad	went down
ask your mom	help her now	on or off	went into
at all	her dad	on the floor	were they
at home	her mom	over and under	what I say
at once	here it is	she can work	what I want
at school	I am	she is pretty	what is that
at three	I am very	she said so	where are you
black and white	I could	she saw me	where can I
by the house	I have a	so long	when I can
by the tree	I know how	so much	when I know
but she said	I like	take for	when did he
but they said	I like school	take from	when you come
can fly	I made it	thank you so much	when you know
can live	I may get	that was fun	who can play
can play	I may go	the funny man	will go
can read	I see	the little children	will look
can run	I was	the little dog	will make
can you	I was on	the yellow ball	will read
come over with	I will come	the yellow cat	will think
could eat	I will get	then he came	will walk
could make	I will go	then he said	with mom
did not fall	if I could	there are blue	with the dog
did not go	if I may	there are many	with us
did you see	if I must	there is	would like
down here	if you can	they are	would want
down there	in the water	they came	yes I can
for him	is coming	they had to	you and I
for the girl	is going	they were	you are
for them	it is	to be there	you saw
from home	it is a new	to go	you were
from the farm	it is about	to stop	you will do
from the tree	it was	to the house	you will like
get them	it was for	to the school	you will see
go to school	just for you	too little	your dad
has come back	just now	too soon	your mom

Reading Sight Words in Context

Highlighting Printed Material: Children love to use highlighters, and they can be an effective tool in helping children focus as they read text. Provide the children with a copy of a story, poem, or even an enlarged article or comic from a newspaper. Give each child a short list of sight words *(no more than five words)* and a highlighter. Have the children search the text for the sight words on the list. When a sight word is found the child should draw a line through it with the highlighter.

Words and Pictures: Children need to know enough words by sight in order to have enough context to help identify other words. Make a variety of sentence strips using sight words and also leave blank spaces for where the nouns will go. Have a variety of noun picture cards available. Let the children practice reading each sentence and placing the noun pictures in the blanks to finish the sentence. Print the word for the noun on the other side of the picture. After reading the sentence with the pictures, the children can turn the cards over and read the sentence again with all of the words.

Another fun variation is to let the children draw their own pictures to go in the blanks. This is a good exercise to make into a paper and pencil task. Create a student page and then copy it for each of the children. Below are several examples to get you started:

Read Predictable Text: Predictable text is an excellent resource for helping children learn to read sight words, and it can also increase fluency. Use children's literature such as, *Brown Bear, Brown Bear, What Do You See?* or *Help Me Find My Cat?* both books by Eric Carle. The following is a step by step approach for using predictable text:

- Show the children the book cover. Discuss aspects of the story before reading it to the children, such as, "What do you think Brown Bear will see?" and "What would a bear see in a forest?" This helps give the children some prior knowledge.

- Read the book to the children. The predictable sentences make good choral reading selections. Encourage the children to say these with you.

- Print the predictable sentences on sentence strips, such as **"Brown bear, brown bear, what do you see?".** Cut the sentence apart and have the children put the words back in order. Provide the children with their own cut-up sentences. Let them rearrange them and glue them back together on a piece of paper.

- Choose another predictable sentence from the story and write it on a sentence strip, such as **"I see a _____ looking at me."** Have the children brainstorm ideas that could be used to fill in the blank. Provide each child with their own cut up sentence. Have each child arrange the sentence and glue it on a piece of paper. Encourage them to draw a picture in the blank. When finished, bind all the children's pages together to create a classroom big book of ***Brown Bear, Brown Bear, What Did You See?*** These books become classroom favorites and are excellent tools for meaningful sight word practice.

Word Wall Activities

The Classroom Word Wall: All the sight words (pages 359–382) should be enlarged, copied, laminated for durability and placed in alphabetical order on the classroom word wall (see #2 on page 8). The word wall is not a display—it is an effective teaching tool to be used daily. It provides daily review of words and how they work, and it provides a reading and writing reference for the children, and it can be incredibly motivational because the children are able to actually see their reading progress as the number of words on the wall keeps increasing!

Here are some word wall suggestions for the teacher to pick and choose from:

1. **Read all the words everyday:** This does not need to be a dull and boring exercise. Make it fun by reading the words using different techniques, such as:

   - **Use chants, rhythms, clapping, tapping, slapping, and snapping.** For example: (slap-slap knees, clap-clap "*W*"), (slap-slap knees, clap-clap "*H*"), (slap-slap knees, clap-clap "*A*"), (slap-slap knees, clap-clap "*T*"), (clap *W* slap, clap *H* slap, clap *A* slap, clap *T* slap.) Yell, "*WHAT*!"

   - **Speed reading:** Read the list slowly the first time and then keep increasing the speed. Time the children with a stop watch. How fast can they read all of the words?

   - **Read the words in funny voices.** How would an alien read the words? How would someone from France, a baby, an old man, or a robot read the words?

   - **Word cheers:** One child is the leader and reads a word (loud - like a cheerleader) and the rest of the class repeats the word. The entire list can be read this way. It is also fun to spell the words using this method.

2. **Play word games:** Learning to read by using games is always fun for young children.

   - **Mystery words:** Look up at the word wall and tell the children that you see a mystery word. Can they figure out which one is the mystery word? Here is an example of clues: The word is on the word wall. The word has four letters. There is an "o" in the word. It begins with the letter "c." I might tell you during recess that, "It is time to _____ inside." Who solved the mystery?

   - **Finish spelling the word:** The teacher chooses a word from the word wall, such as the word "run." The teacher says the word "run" and the letter "r" — and the children should finish spelling it by saying "u - n." As another example, the teacher would say the word "yellow" and then she might spell " y - e," and the children would respond with "l - l - o - w."

   - **Which word makes sense:** The teacher chooses four words that begin with the same letter. The children write those words on a piece of paper. Next the teacher says a sentence but leaves out one word. The children need to decide which of the four words they have written down will work best to complete the sentence.

   - **Letter tiles or letter cards:** Each child will need a set of letter cards. The teacher then chooses several words from the word wall. She says a word and then have the children spell the word using their letter cards.

   - **Children's Own Word Wall Dictionaries:** Each child should make their own word wall dictionary. Each child will need a journal or spiral bound notebook. In alphabetical order, the children should write a letter in the top right-hand corner of each page. Each time a new sight word is introduced, have the children write the word on the correct page of their own dictionaries. For example, jump would be written down on the "J" page.

See. Say. Rainbow trace.
-1-

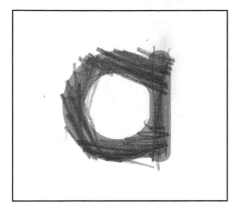 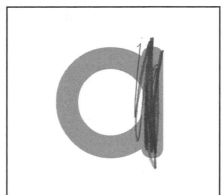 

Cut and Paste. -2-

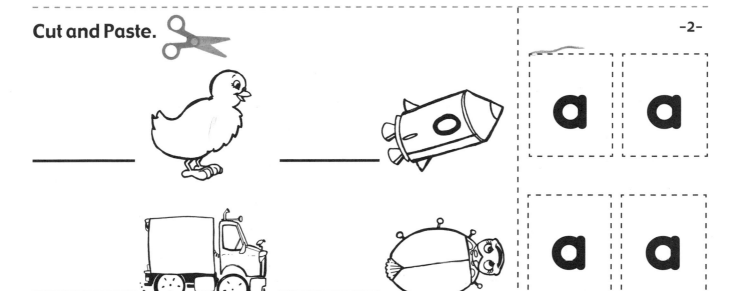

Trace and print. -3-

_____ _____ _____ _____ _____ _____

TIC-TAC-TOE
Circle the " a " letters.

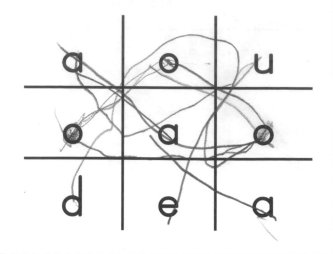

Circle every letter "a" in the snake.

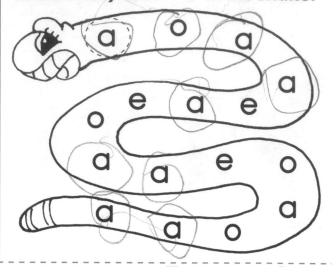

COLOR THE LETTERS
Decorate each letter " a."

FINISH THE SENTENCE
Use the word " a" to fill in the blanks. Read each sentence. Draw a picture.

1. This is _____ cat

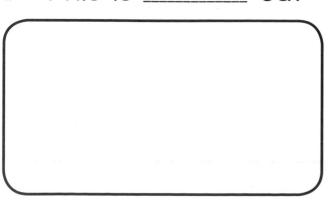

2. I see _____ bird.

See. Say. Rainbow trace.

about

Cut and Paste.

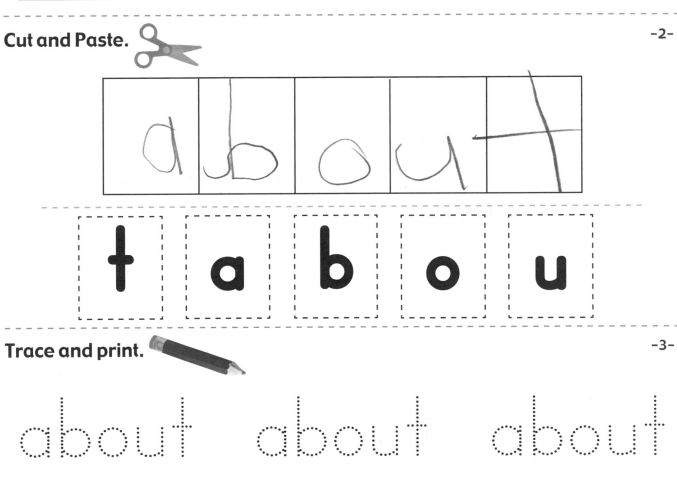

about

t a b o u

Trace and print.

about   about   about

WORD SEARCH
Circle the words "about."

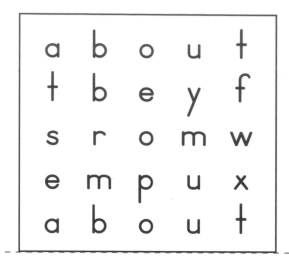

a	b	o	u	t
t	b	e	y	f
s	r	o	m	w
e	m	p	u	x
a	b	o	u	t

PYRAMID WORDS
Build a pyramid for the word "about."

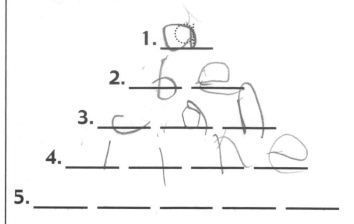

1. _____
2. _____
3. _____
4. _____
5. _____

(The first letter goes on the top line. The first and second letters go on the second line and so on.)

SCRAMBLED WORDS: Unscramble the letters to spell the word "about."   –5–

utboa   uobat   atubo   baotu

_____   _____   _____   _____

SPELL IT! Circle all the words that spell "about."   –6–

about
around

about
above

about
away

again
about

about
after

See. Say. Rainbow trace.

Cut and Paste.

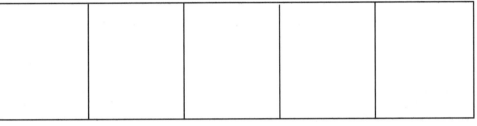

e a r t f

Trace and print.

 after after after

BLEND THE WORD
Draw a line to make the word "after."

WORD TIC-TAC-TOE
Circle the words "after."

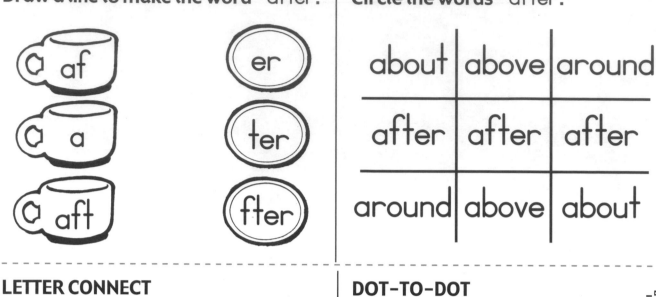

about	above	around
after	after	after
around	above	about

LETTER CONNECT
Connect the letters that spell "after."

DOT-TO-DOT
Connect the letters that spell "after."

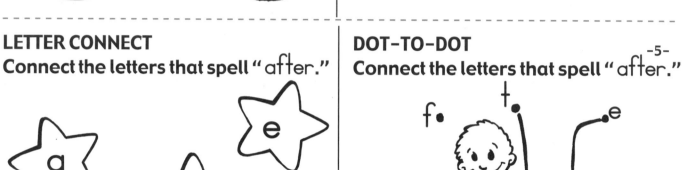

FINISH THE SENTENCE
Use the word "after" to fill in the blanks. Read each sentence.

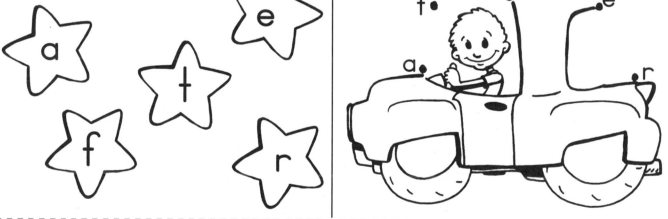

1. We ran _____ the dog.

2. We will play _____ lunch.

3. Let's play _____ school.

See. Say. Rainbow trace.

Cut and Paste.

i   a   a   n   g

Trace and print.

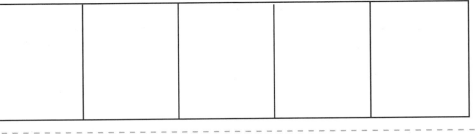

again   again   again

_____   _____   _____

WORD TIC-TAC-TOE
Circle the words "again."

above	after	around
above	after	above
again	again	again

LETTER MAZE
Circle the letters to spell "again."

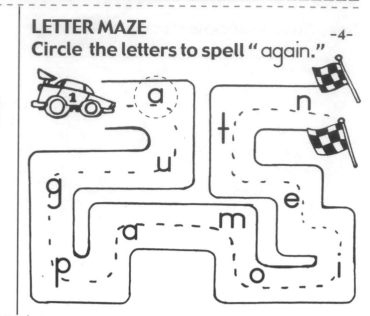

MISSING LETTERS: Fill in the missing letters for the word "again."

g ___ ___ i

___ g ___ ___ n

a ___ ___ ___ n

a ___ ___ ___ i

COLORING WORDS: Color all of the sections that have the word "again."

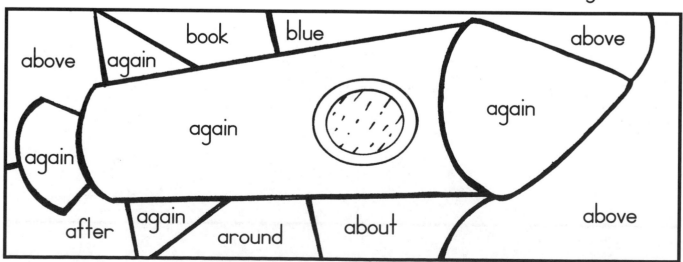

See. Say. Rainbow trace.

Cut and Paste.

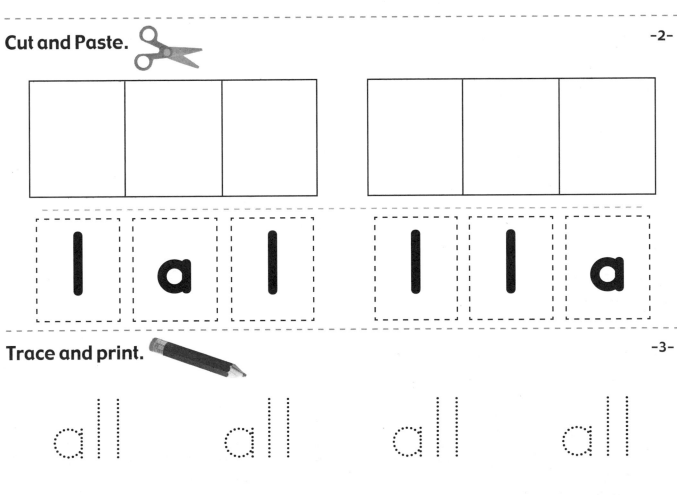

Trace and print. -3-

all   all   all   all

WORD SEARCH
Circle the words "all."

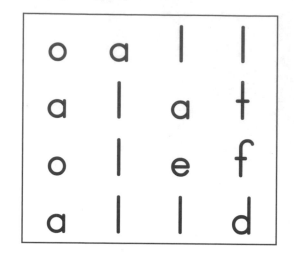

o	a	l	l
a	l	a	t
o	l	e	f
a	l	l	d

PYRAMID WORDS
Build a pyramid for the word "all." -4-

1. ___a___

2. ___ ___

3. ___ ___ ___

SCRAMBLED WORDS: Unscramble the letters to spell the word "all." -5-

lal   lla   lal   lla

___   ___   ___   ___

COLORING WORDS: Color all of the train sections that have the word "all." -6-

See. Say. Rainbow trace.

Cut and Paste.

m | a   m | a

Trace and print.

am   am   am   am

BLEND THE WORD
Draw a line to make the word "am."

at	an	as
am	am	am
an	at	an

LETTER CONNECT
Connect the letters that spell "am."

FINISH THE SENTENCE
Use the word "am" to fill in the blanks. Read each sentence.

1. I _____ very tall.

2. I _____ a good boy.

3. I _____ going to school.

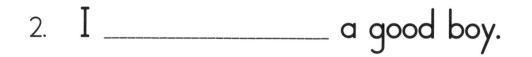

See. Say. Rainbow trace.

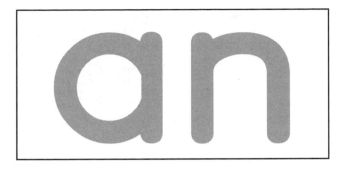

Cut and Paste. ✂

n	a		n	a	

Trace and print. ✏

an   an   an   an

_____ _____ _____ _____

WORD TIC-TAC-TOE
Circle the words "an."

an	at	as
at	an	am
as	am	an

WORD MAZE
Circle the words that spell "an."

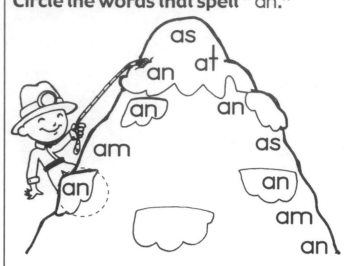

MISSING LETTERS: Fill in the missing letters for the word "an."

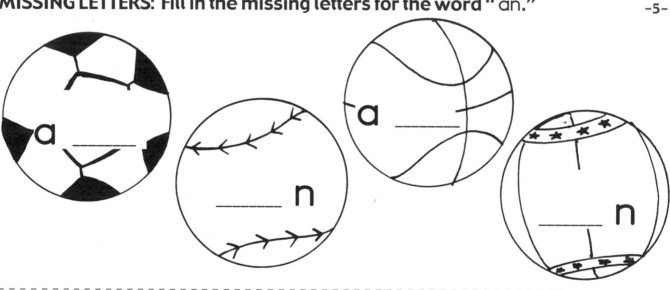

COLORING WORDS: Color all of the lily pads that have the word "an."

and

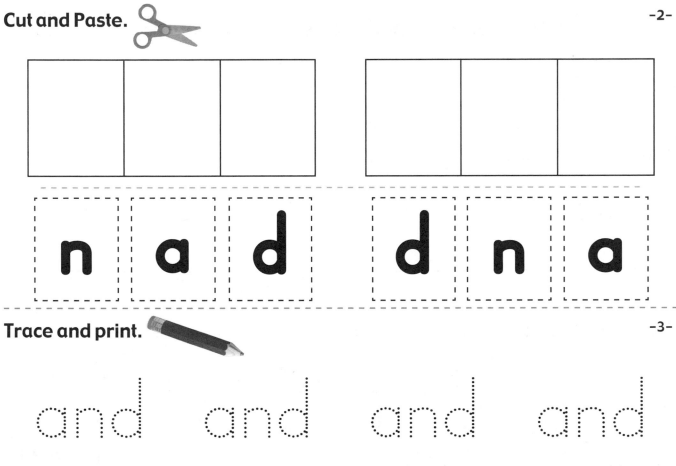

n	a	d	d	n	a

and   and   and   and

_____ _____ _____ _____

WORD SEARCH
Circle the words "and."

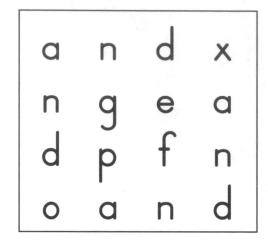

a	n	d	x
n	g	e	a
d	p	f	n
o	a	n	d

PYRAMID WORDS
-4-

Build a pyramid for the word "and."

1. ___a___

2. _____ _____

3. _____ _____ _____

SCRAMBLED WORDS: Unscramble the letters to spell the word "and."
-5-

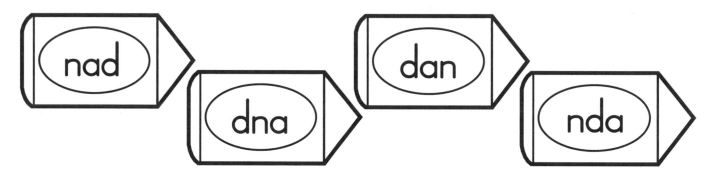

nad

dna

dan

nda

_____ _____ _____ _____

COLORING WORDS: Color all of the books that have the word "and."
-6-

See. Say. Rainbow trace. -1-

Cut and Paste. ✂ -2-

| n | a y | | y a | n |

Trace and print. ✏ -3-

any   any   any   any

_____ _____ _____ _____

BLEND THE WORD
Draw a line to make the word "any."

TIC-TAC-TOE
Circle the letters that spell "any."

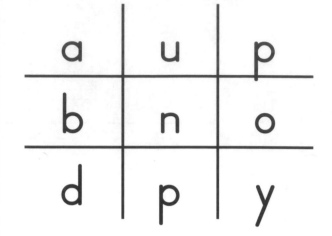

a	u	p
b	n	o
d	p	y

LETTER MAZE
Circle the letters that spell "any."

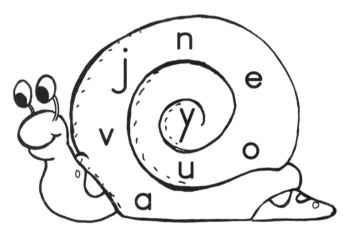

DOT-TO-DOT
Connect the letters that spell "any."

FINISH THE SENTENCE
Use the word "any" to fill in the blanks. Read each sentence.

1. I do not have _____ .

2. Are there _____ more?

3. Do you have _____ cookies?

are

Cut and Paste. ✂ -2-

r a e   a e r

Trace and print. ✏ -3-

are   are   are   are

——————— ——————— ——————— ———————

TIC-TAC-TOE
Circle the letters that spell "are."

a	r	e
n	u	t
y	n	m

LETTER MAZE
Circle the letters that spell "are."

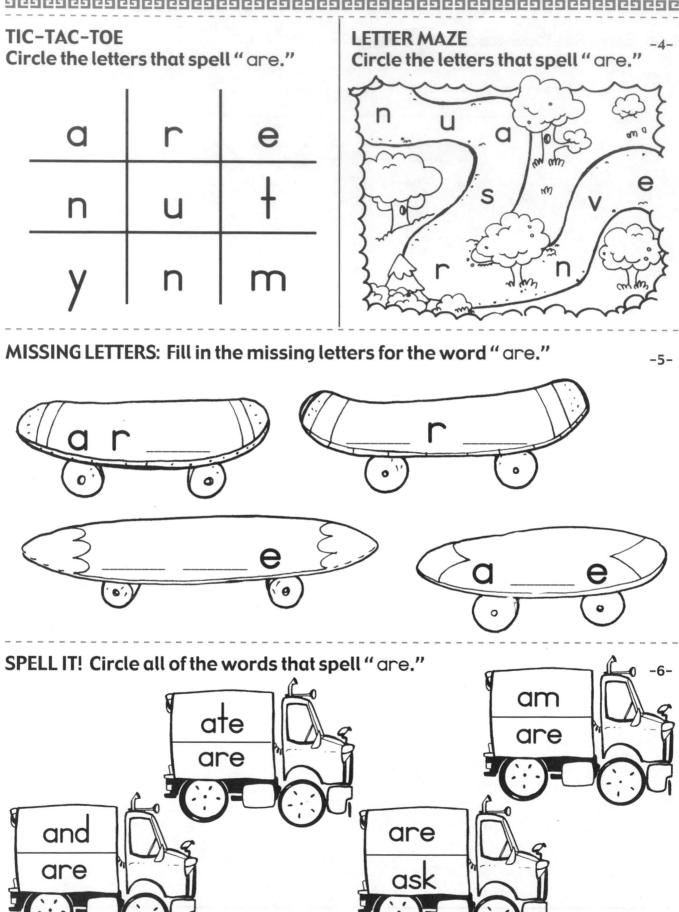

MISSING LETTERS: Fill in the missing letters for the word "are."

a r ____

____ r ____

____ ____ e

a ____ e

SPELL IT! Circle all of the words that spell "are."

ate
are

am
are

and
are

are
ask

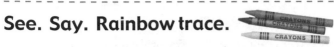

Cut and Paste. ✂ -2-

| s | a | | s | a |

Trace and print. ✏ -3-

as   as   as   as

_____ _____ _____ _____

WORD SEARCH
Circle the words "as."

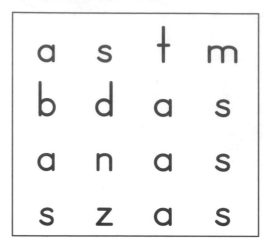

a s t m
b d a s
a n a s
s z a s

PYRAMID WORDS
-4-
Build a pyramid for the word "as."

1. ___ a ___

2. _____ _____

(The first letter goes on the top line. The first and second letters go on the second line and so on.)

SCRAMBLED WORDS: Unscramble the letters to spell the word "as." -5-

sa sa sa sa

_____ _____ _____ _____

COLORING WORDS: Color all of the book covers that have the word "as." -6-

an as   as in

as at   as is   is as

See. Say. Rainbow trace.

Cut and Paste. ✂

| s | a | k | | k | s | a |

Trace and print. ✏

ask   ask   ask   ask

_____ _____ _____ _____

BLEND THE WORD
Draw a line to make the word "ask."

TIC-TAC-TOE
-4-
Circle the letters that spell "ask."

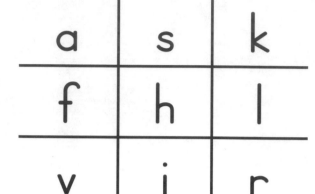

a	s	k
f	h	l
v	i	r

LETTER CONNECT
Connect the letters that spell "ask."

DOT-TO-DOT
-5-
Connect the letters that spell "ask."

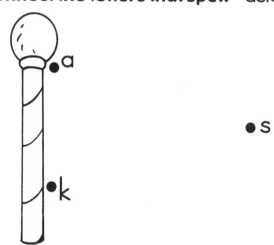

FINISH THE SENTENCE
-6-
Use the word "ask" to fill in the blanks. Read each sentence.

1. I will _____ my mom.

2. Did you _____ him to play?

3. Let's _____ if we can go too.

See. Say. Rainbow trace.

at

Cut and Paste.

t   a   t   a

Trace and print.

at   at   at   at

_____   _____   _____   _____

WORD TIC-TAC-TOE
Circle the words "at."

at	as	an
an	at	am
am	as	at

WORD MAZE
Circle the words that spell "at."

MISSING LETTERS: Fill in the missing letters for the word "at." — -5-

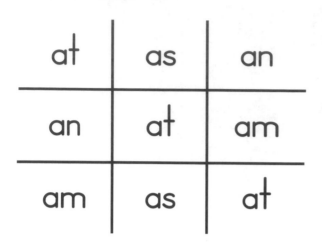

COLORING WORDS: Color all of the ducks that have the word "at." — -6-

See. Say. Rainbow trace.

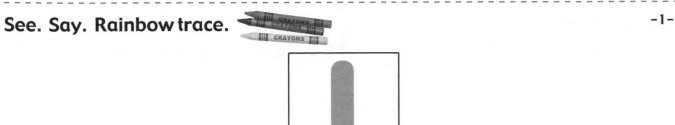

Cut and Paste.

| a | e | t | | t | e | a |

Trace and print.

ate   ate   ate   ate

———————   ———————   ———————   ———————

WORD SEARCH
Circle the words "ate."

a	t	e	e	a
a	f	l	t	t
a	t	u	n	e
e	e	a	t	e

PYRAMID WORDS
-4-
Build a pyramid for the word "ate."

1. ___a___

2. ___ ___

3. ___ ___ ___

(The first letter goes on the top line. The first and second letters go on the second line and so on.)

SCRAMBLED WORDS: Unscramble the letters to spell the word "ate." -5-

eat   tea   aet   tae

___ ___ ___ ___

COLORING WORDS: Color all of the wings that have the word "ate." -6-

ate   at   all   ate   am   ate

eat   ate   ate   and   ate   end

See. Say. Rainbow trace.

Cut and Paste. ✂ -2-

y   a   w   a

Trace and print. -3-

away   away   away

_____   _____   _____

BLEND THE WORD
Draw a line to make the word "away."

WORD TIC-TAC-TOE
Circle the words " away."

away	away	away
and	above	after
after	about	are

LETTER CONNECT
Connect the letters that spell " away."

DOT-TO-DOT
Connect the letters that spell " away."

FINISH THE SENTENCE
Use the word " away" to fill in the blanks. Read each sentence.

1. The dog ran _____ .

2. He went _____ .

3. Did she go _____ ?

     The Best Sight Word Book Ever!

See. Say. Rainbow trace.

ball

Cut and Paste.

l   b   l   a

Trace and print.

ball   ball   ball   ball

_____   _____   _____   _____

WORD TIC-TAC-TOE
Circle the words "ball."

ball	hall	call
mall	ball	tall
fall	doll	ball

LETTER MAZE
Circle the letters that spell the word "ball."

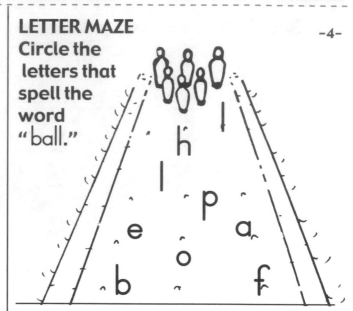

MISSING LETTERS: Fill in the missing letters for the word "ball."

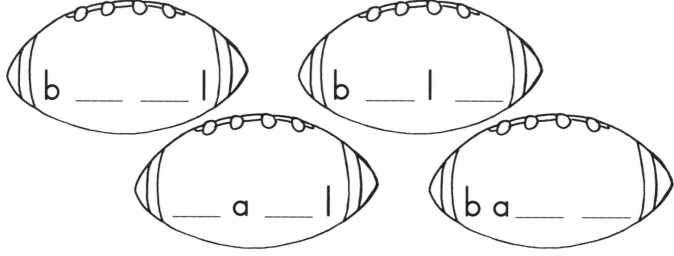

COLORING WORDS: Color all of the balls that have the word "ball."

See. Say. Rainbow trace.

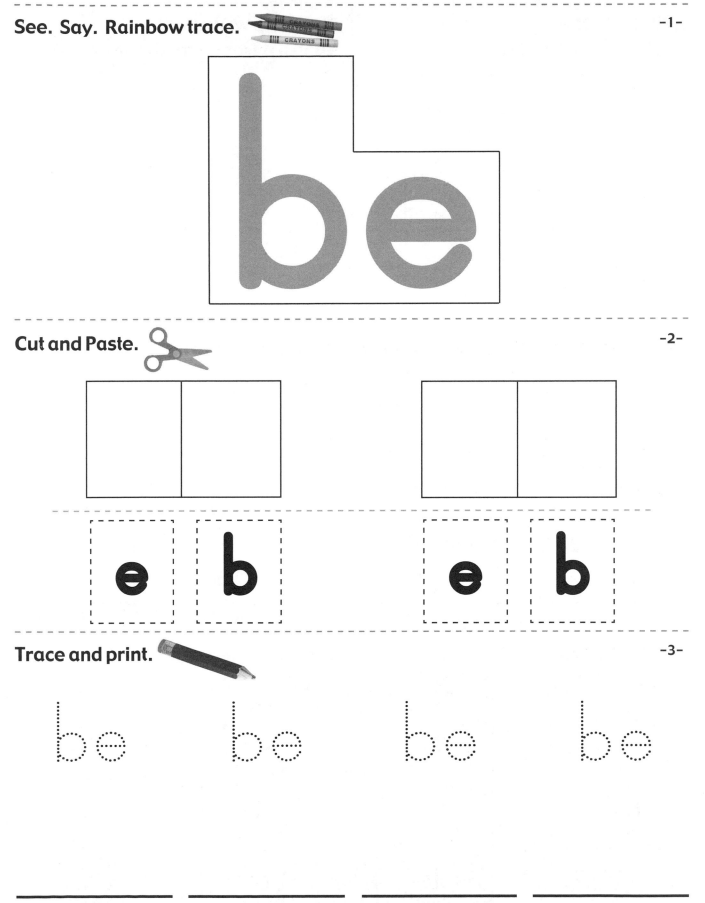

Cut and Paste.

Trace and print. -3-

be   be   be   be

WORD SEARCH
Circle the words "be."

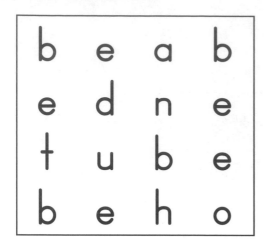

b e a b a b
e d n e
e d n e
t u b e
b e h o

PYRAMID WORDS
Build a pyramid for the word "be."

-4-

1. ___b___

2. _____ _____

(The first letter goes on the top line. The first and second letters go on the second line and so on.)

MISSING LETTERS: Fill in the missing letters for the word "be."

-5-

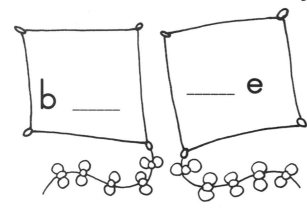 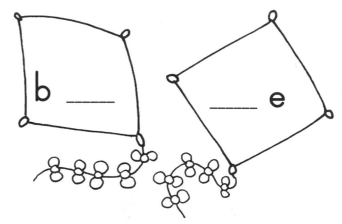

b ___   ___ e   b ___   ___ e

_____ _____ _____ _____

COLORING WORDS: Color all of the circles that have the word "be."

-6-

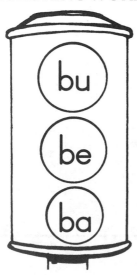 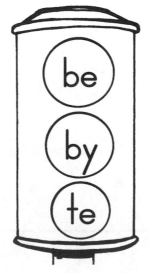 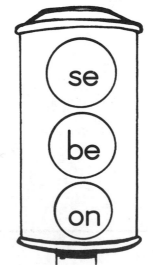 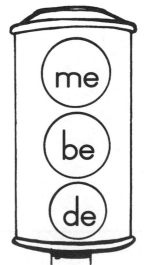

bu	be	se	me
be	by	be	be
ba	te	on	de

See. Say. Rainbow trace.

Cut and Paste.

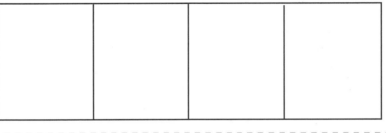

Trace and print.

been   been   been

BLEND THE WORD
Draw a line to make the word "been."

b
be
bee

een
n
en

WORD TIC-TAC-TOE
Circle the words "been."

been	ball	above
be	been	ball
be	above	been

LETTER CONNECT
Connect the letters that spell "been."

b
e
n
e

DOT-TO-DOT
Connect the letters that spell "been."

e
e
b
n

FINISH THE SENTENCE
Use the word "been" to fill in the blanks. Read each sentence.

1. I have _____ to school.

2. Where have you _____ ?

3. We have _____ to the zoo.

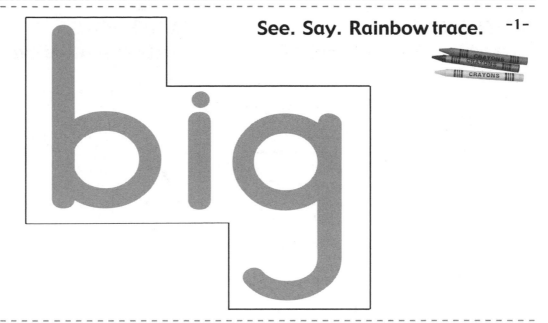

Cut and Paste. -2-

b	g	i	i	b	g

Trace and print. -3-

big   big   big   big

_____ _____ _____ _____

TIC-TAC-TOE
Circle the letters that spell "big."

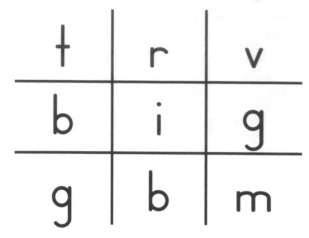

t	r	v
b	i	g
g	b	m

LETTER MAZE
-4-
Circle the letters that spell "big."

MISSING LETTERS: Fill in the missing letters for the word "big."
-5-

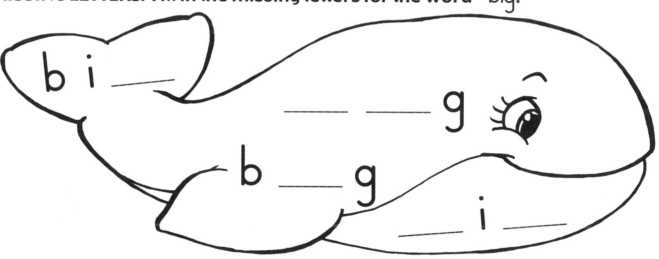

COLORING WORDS: Color all of the sections that have the word "big."
-6-

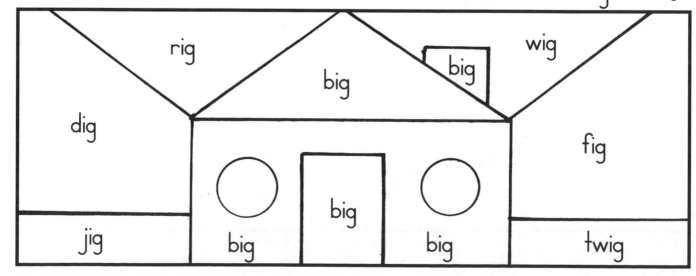

See. Say. Rainbow trace.

Cut and Paste. ✂

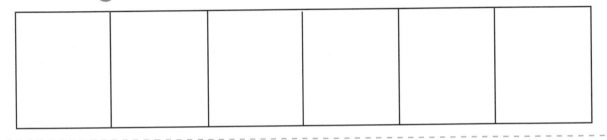

| l | a | b | k | c |

Trace and print. ✏

black   black   black

_____   _____   _____

WORD SEARCH
Circle the words "black."

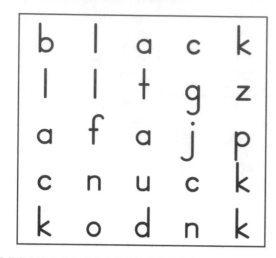

b	l	a	c	k
l	l	t	g	z
a	f	a	j	p
c	n	u	c	k
k	o	d	n	k

PYRAMID WORDS
-4-
Build a pyramid for the word "black."

1. b ___
2. ___ ___
3. ___ ___ ___
4. ___ ___ ___ ___
5. ___ ___ ___ ___ ___

(The first letter goes on the top line. The first and second letters go on the second line and so on.)

SCRAMBLED WORDS: Unscramble the letters to spell the word "black." -5-

lbcak   kbcla   kbcla   clakb

___ ___ ___ ___

COLORING WORDS: Color all of the sections that have the word "black." -6-

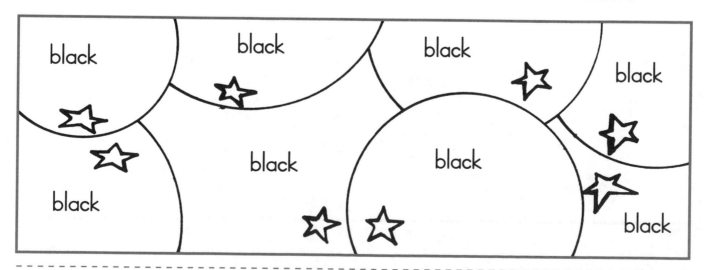

See. Say. Rainbow trace.

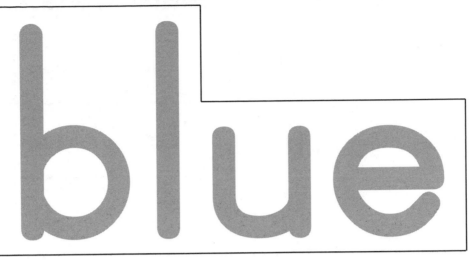

Cut and Paste.

l   b   e   u

Trace and print.

blue   blue   blue   blue

BLEND THE WORD
Draw a line to make the word "blue."

 blu

 lue

b

e

bl

ue

WORD TIC-TAC-TOE
Circle the words "blue."

be	been	black
big	black	been
blue	blue	blue

LETTER CONNECT
Connect the letters that spell "blue."

DOT-TO-DOT
Connect the letters that spell "blue."

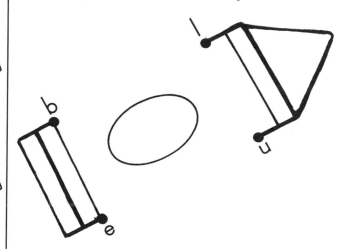

FINISH THE SENTENCE
Use the word "blue" to fill in the blanks. Read each sentence.

1. I have a _____ hat.

2. My room is the color _____ .

3. Look at the _____ sky.

**See. Say.
Rainbow trace.**

Cut and Paste.

o b y   y b o

Trace and print.

boy   boy   boy   boy

_____   _____   _____   _____

TIC-TAC-TOE
Circle the letters that spell "boy."

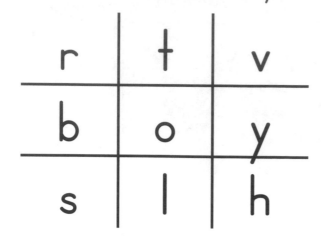

r	t	v
b	o	y
s	l	h

LETTER MAZE
Circle the letters that spell "boy."

MISSING LETTERS: Fill in the missing letters for the word "boy."   -5-

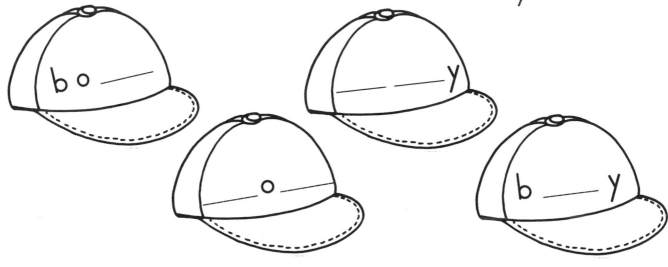

b o ____

____ y

o

b ____ y

COLORING WORDS: Color each sign that has the word "boy."   -6-

boy   day   toy   boy   hoy   boy   joy   boy

See. Say. Rainbow trace.

brown

Cut and Paste. ✂

r   n   b   o   w

Trace and print. ✏

brown   brown   brown

_____   _____   _____

WORD SEARCH
Circle the words "brown."

b	r	o	w	n	b
p	b	m	d	w	r
q	r	r	z	v	o
u	o	m	o	x	w
s	w	k	p	w	n
e	n	u	x	v	n

PYRAMID WORDS   -4-
Build a pyramid for the word "brown."

1. _b_

2. ___ ___

3. ___ ___ ___

4. ___ ___ ___ ___

5. ___ ___ ___ ___ ___

(The first letter goes on the top line. The first and second letters go on the second line and so on.)

SCRAMBLED WORDS: Unscramble the letters to spell the word "brown."   -5-

rowbn   robwn   bnowr   worbn

_____ _____ _____ _____

COLORING WORDS: Color all of the bears that have the word "brown."   -6-

brown   brown   bruwn   brown

See. Say. Rainbow trace.

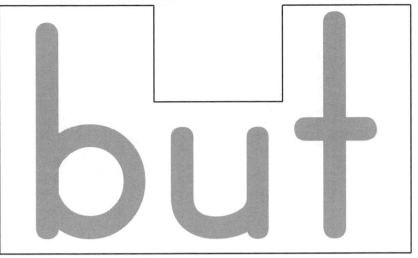

Cut and Paste. ✂

t	u	b		b	t	u

Trace and print. ✏

but   but   but   but

_____   _____   _____   _____

BLEND THE WORD
Draw a line to make the word "but."

TIC-TAC-TOE
Circle the letters that spell "but."

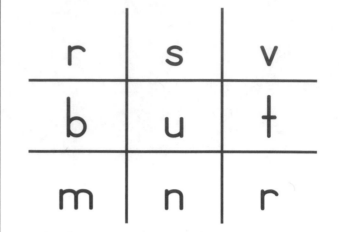

r	s	v
b	u	t
m	n	r

LETTER MAZE
Circle the letters that spell "but."

DOT-TO-DOT
Connect the letters that spell "but."

FINISH THE SENTENCE
Use the word "but" to fill in the blanks. Read each sentence.

1. Yes, _____ not now.

2. I cannot go, _____ you can.

3. I ran, _____ I fell down.

See. Say. Rainbow trace. 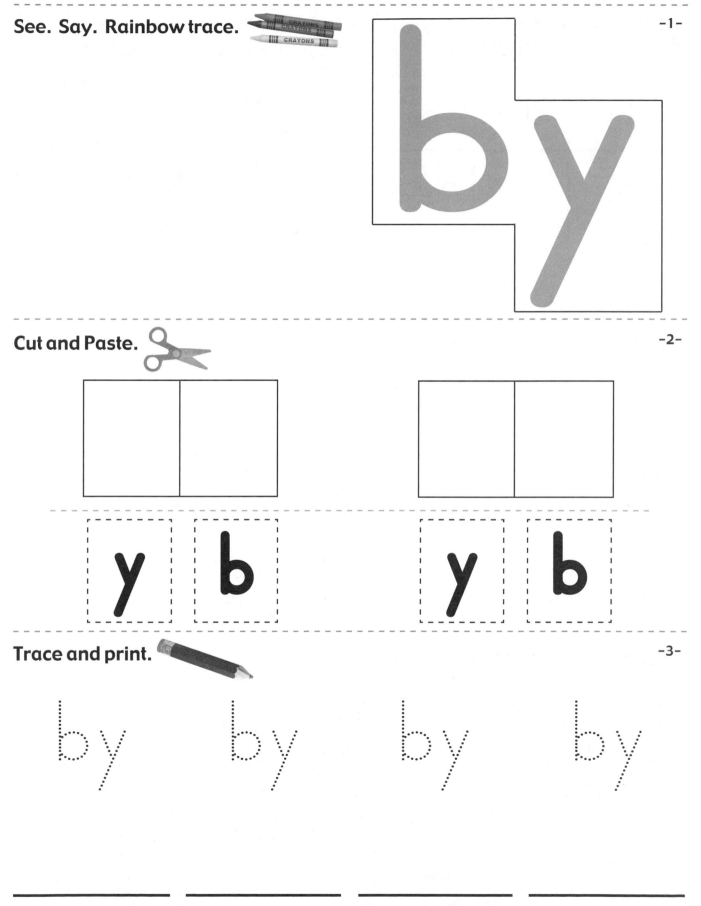 -1-

Cut and Paste. -2-

y   b   y   b

Trace and print. -3-

by   by   by   by

_____ _____ _____ _____

WORD TIC-TAC-TOE
Circle the words "by."

by	blue	be
by	been	black
by	big	be

WORD MAZE: Circle the words "by." How many did you find?

-4-

_____

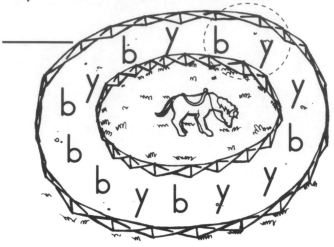

MISSING LETTERS: Fill in the missing letters for the word "by."

-5-

b ___   ___ y   b ___   ___ y

SPELL IT! Circle all of the words that spell "by."

-6-

by   ty   by   dy

sy   by   by   fy

See. Say. Rainbow trace.

call

Cut and Paste.

l c l a

Trace and print.

call   call   call   call

_____   _____   _____   _____

WORD SEARCH
Circle the words " call."

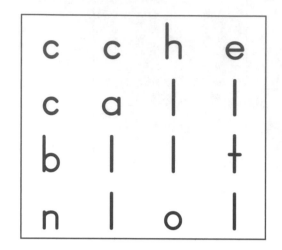

c	c	h	e
c	a	l	l
b	l	l	t
n	l	o	l

PYRAMID WORDS
-4-
Build a pyramid for the word " call."

1. __c__

2. _____ _____

3. _____ _____ _____

4. _____ _____ _____ _____

(The first letter goes on the top line. The first and second letters go on the second line and so on.)

SCRAMBLED WORDS: Unscramble the letters to spell the word " call."   -5-

allc   clal   llca   lcal

_____ _____ _____ _____

COLORING WORDS: Color all of the wheels that have the word " call."   -6-

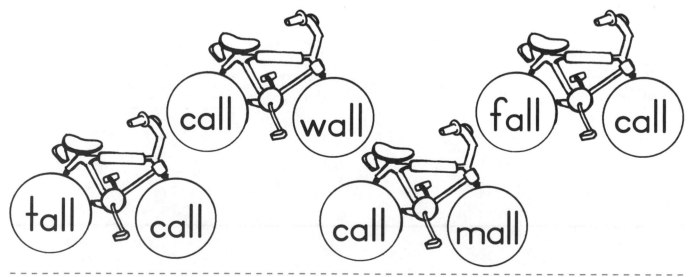

call   wall   fall   call

tall   call   call   mall

See. Say. Rainbow trace.

Cut and Paste.

m   c   a   e

Trace and print.

came   came   came

BLEND THE WORD
Draw a line to make the word "came."

ca   ame

c   me

cam   e

WORD TIC-TAC-TOE   -4-
Circle the words "came."

can	call	came
could	come	came
come	can	came

LETTER MAZE
Circle the letters that spell "came."

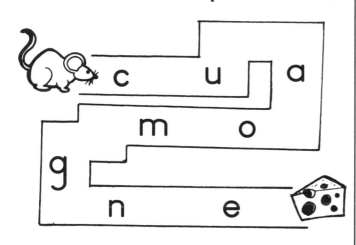

c   u   a
m   o
g
n   e

DOT-TO-DOT   -5-
Connect the letters that spell "came."

c   e

a
         m

FINISH THE SENTENCE   -6-
Use the word "came" to fill in the blanks. Read each sentence.

1. He _____ home.

2. She _____ to my house.

3. The boy _____ to school.

Cut and Paste. ✂ -2-

a	c	n		n	c	a

Trace and print. ✏ -3-

can   can   can   can

_____ _____ _____ _____

TIC-TAC-TOE
Circle the letters that spell " can."

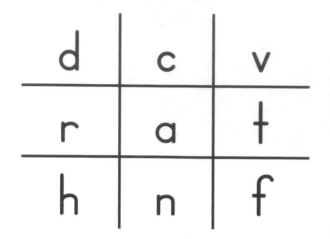

LETTER MAZE
Circle the letters that spell " can."

MISSING LETTERS: Fill in the missing letters for the word " can."

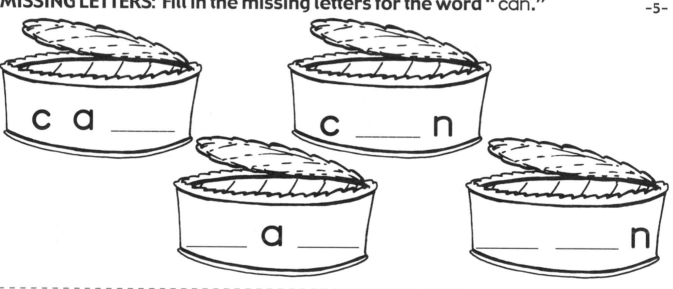

SPELL IT! Color all of the cans that have the word " can."

See. Say. Rainbow trace.

Cut and Paste.

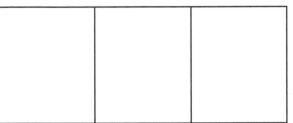 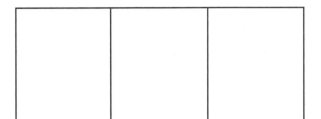

a	c	t

t	c	a

Trace and print.

cat   cat   cat   cat

_____   _____   _____   _____

WORD SEARCH
Circle the words "cat."

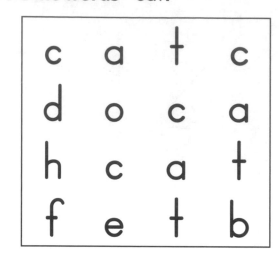

```
c a t c
d o c a
h c a t
f e t b
```

PYRAMID WORDS -4-
Build a pyramid for the word "cat."

1. ___C___

2. _____ _____

3. _____ _____ _____

(The first letter goes on the top line. The first and second letters go on the second line and so on.)

SCRAMBLED WORDS: Unscramble the letters to spell the word "cat." -5-

tca   atc   cta   act

_____   _____

COLORING WORDS: Color all of the sections that have the word "cat." -6-

come

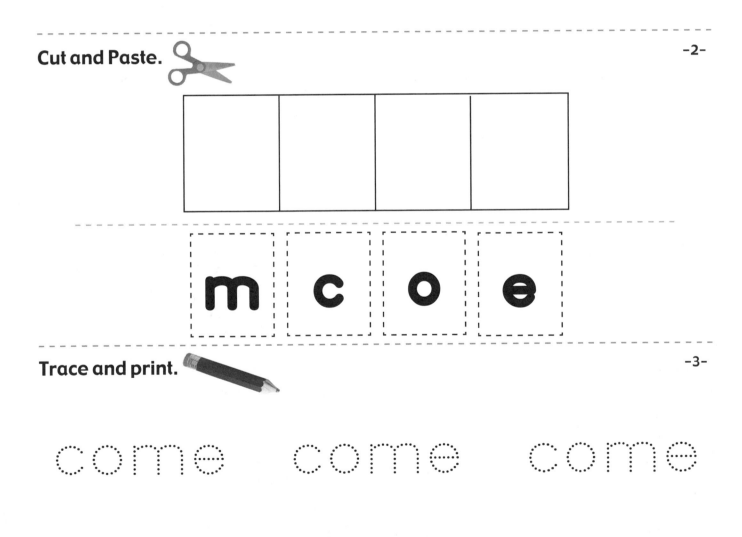

m c o e

come   come   come

_____   _____   _____

BLEND THE WORD
Draw a line to make the word "come."

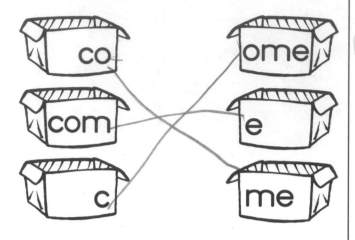

WORD TIC-TAC-TOE
Circle the words "come."

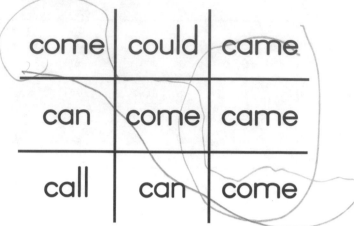

LETTER CONNECT
Connect the letters that spell "come."

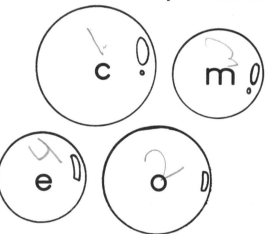

DOT-TO-DOT
Connect the letters that spell "come."

FINISH THE SENTENCE
Use the word "come" to fill in the blanks. Read each sentence.

1. Did father __come__ home?

2. Where did he __come__ from?

3. Please __come__ here.

See. Say. Rainbow trace.

Cut and Paste.

d c l o u

Trace and print.

could   could   could

WORD TIC-TAC-TOE
Circle the words " could."

would	come	can
can	came	should
could	could	could

LETTER MAZE
-4-
Circles the letters that spell " could."

MISSING LETTERS: Fill in the missing letters for the word " could."
-5-

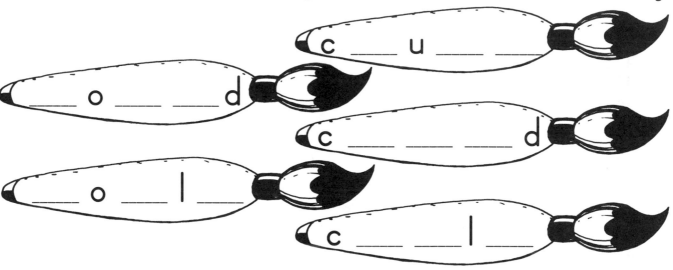

c ___ u ___ ___

___ o ___ ___ d

c ___ ___ ___ ___ d

___ ___ o ___ l ___

c ___ ___ ___ l ___

COLORING WORDS: Color all of the mittens that have the word " could."
-6-

could   come   came   could

should   could   could   would

See. Say. Rainbow trace.

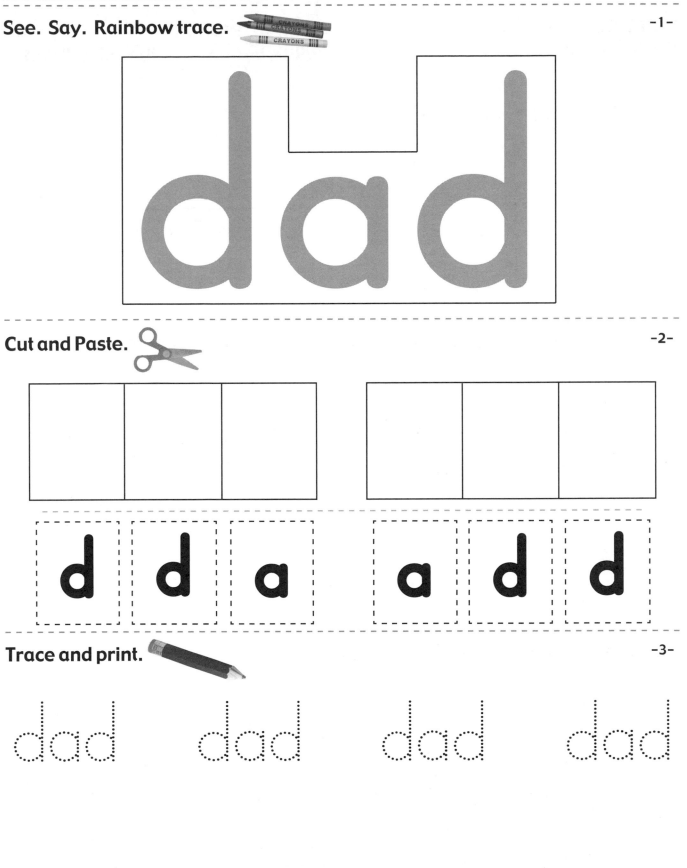

Cut and Paste.

Trace and print.

-81-

WORD SEARCH
Circle the words "dad."

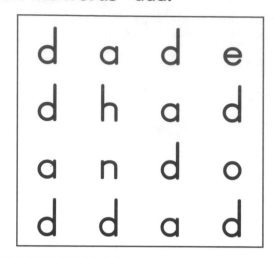

d	a	d	e
d	h	a	d
a	n	d	o
d	d	a	d

PYRAMID WORDS
Build a pyramid for the word "dad."

-4-

1. ___d___

2. _____ _____

3. _____ _____ _____

(The first letter goes on the top line. The first and second letters go on the second line and so on.)

SCRAMBLED WORDS: Unscramble the letters to spell the word "dad."

-5-

dda   add   add   dda

_____ _____ _____ _____

COLORING WORDS: Color all of the chairs that have the word "dad."

-6-

day

Cut and Paste. -2-

a d y   y d a

Trace and print. -3-

day day day day

_____ _____ _____ _____

BLEND THE WORD
Draw a line to make the word "day."

TIC-TAC-TOE
Circle the letters that spell "day."

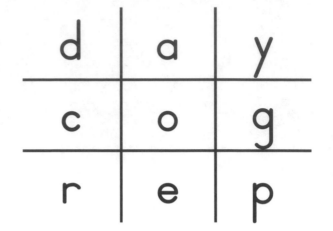

LETTER CONNECT
Connect the letters that spell "day."

DOT-TO-DOT
Connect the letters that spell "day."

FINISH THE SENTENCE
Use the word "day" to fill in the blanks. Read each sentence.

1. What _____ is it?

2. My _____ was fun.

3. Where did the _____ go?

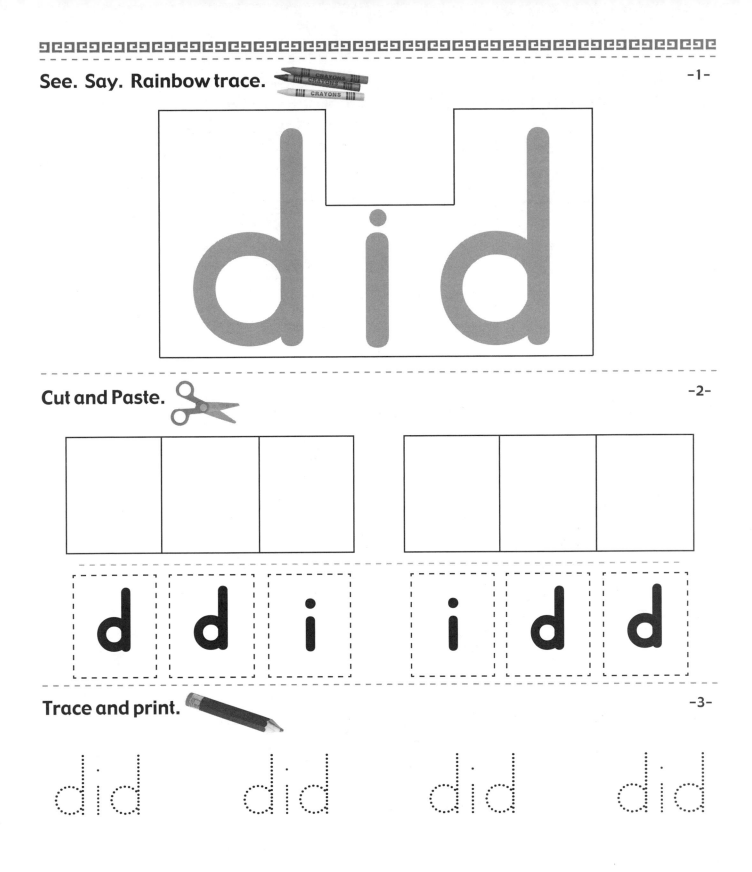

See. Say. Rainbow trace.

-1-

did

Cut and Paste.

-2-

d   d   i   i   d   d

Trace and print.

-3-

did   did   did   did

TIC-TAC-TOE
Circle the letters that spell "did."

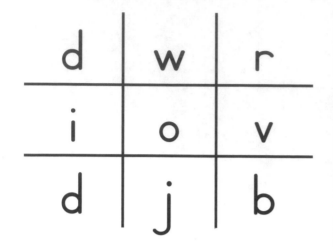

d	w	r
i	o	v
d	j	b

WORD MAZE:
Circle the words "did." How many did you find?

_____

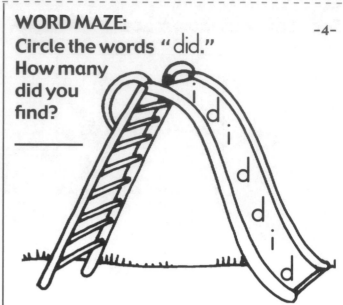

MISSING LETTERS: Fill in the missing letters for the word "did."

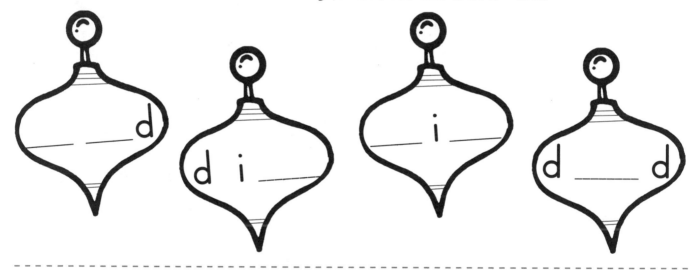

COLORING WORDS! Color all of the sections that have the word "did."

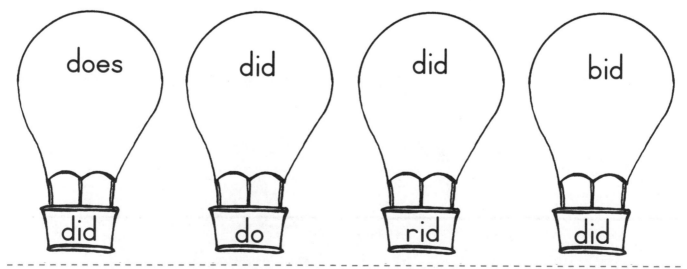

See. Say. Rainbow trace.

do

Cut and Paste.

o d   o d

Trace and print.

do   do   do   do

_____ _____ _____ _____

WORD SEARCH
Circle the words " do."

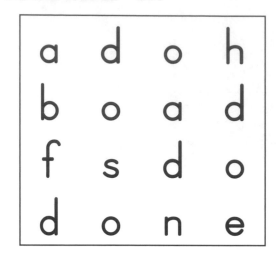

a d o h
b o a d
f s d o
d o n e

PYRAMID WORDS
Build a pyramid for the word " do." −4−

1. ___d___

2. _____ _____

(The first letter goes on the top line. The first and second letters go on the second line and so on.)

MISSING LETTERS: Fill in the missing letters for the word " do." −5−

d___   ___o   ___o   d___

WORD MAZE −6−
Circle all of the words that spell " do."

The Best Sight Word Book Ever!

dog

**See. Say.
Rainbow trace.**

Cut and Paste.

o   d   g   g   d   o

Trace and print.

dog   dog   dog   dog

BLEND THE WORD
Draw a line to make the word "dog."

TIC-TAC-TOE
Circle the letters that spell "dog." -4-

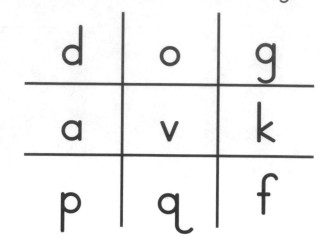

WORD MAZE
Circle all of the words that spell "dog."

DOT-TO-DOT
Connect the letters that spell "dog." -5-

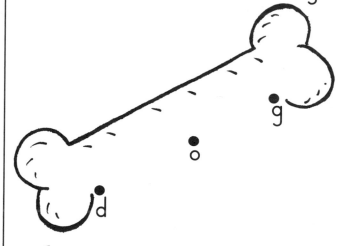

FINISH THE SENTENCE
Use the word "dog" to fill in the blanks. Read each sentence. -6-

1. I have a new _____ .

2. My _____ likes to run.

3. My _____ wants some water.

See. Say. Rainbow trace.

Cut and Paste.

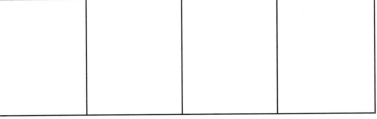

o n d w

Trace and print.

down   down   down

WORD TIC-TAC-TOE
Circle the words "down."

dog	blue	down
did	down	brown
down	black	dog

LETTER MAZE
Circle the letters that spell "down."

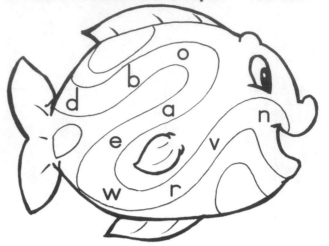

MISSING LETTERS: Fill in the missing letters for the word "down."

COLORING WORDS: Color all the submarines that have the word "down." -6-

See. Say. Rainbow trace.

Cut and Paste.

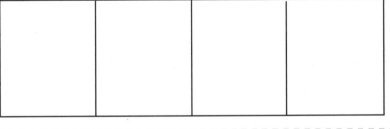

a e h c

Trace and print.

each   each   each

WORD SEARCH
Circle the words "each."

e	e	a	c	h
a	e	d	e	n
c	h	a	a	v
h	n	m	c	f
b	f	b	h	h

PYRAMID WORDS
Build a pyramid for the word "each."

-4-

1. __e__

2. ___ ___

3. ___ ___ ___

4. ___ ___ ___ ___

(The first letter goes on the top line. The first and second letters go on the second line and so on.)

SCRAMBLED WORDS: Unscramble the letters to spell the word "each."

-5-

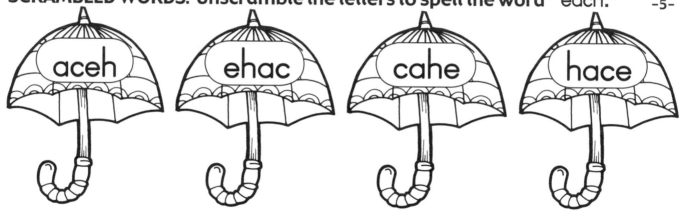

aceh   ehac   cahe   hace

_____   _____

COLORING WORDS
Color all of the raindrops that have the word "each."

-6-

each   each   five

each   eat   each   each   eight   each

See. Say. Rainbow trace.

Cut and Paste.

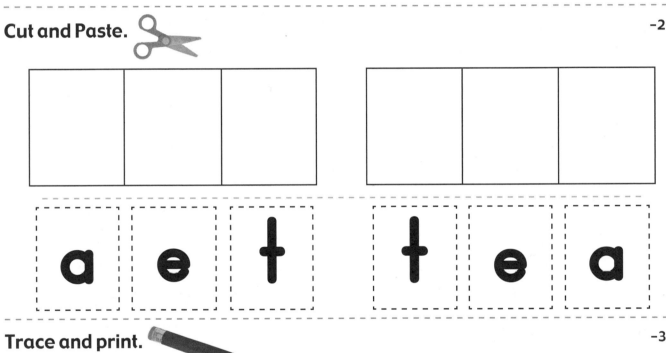

Trace and print.

eat   eat   eat   eat

BLEND THE WORD
Draw a line to make the word "eat."

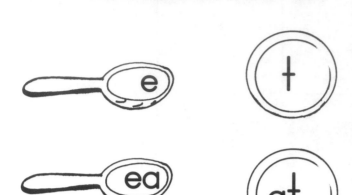

TIC-TAC-TOE
Circle the letters that spell "eat."

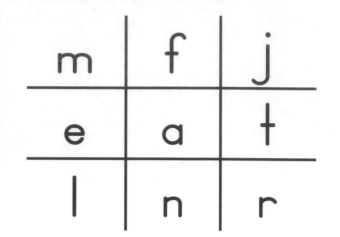

m	f	j
e	a	t
l	n	r

LETTER CONNECT
Connect the letters that spell "eat."

DOT-TO-DOT
Connect the letters that spell "eat."

FINISH THE SENTENCE

Use the word "eat" to fill in the blanks. Read each sentence.

1. We should _____ lunch.

2. I will _____ an apple.

3. Do you want to _____ ?

See. Say. Rainbow trace.

eight

Cut and Paste.

i   h   e   t   g

Trace and print.

eight   eight   eight

WORD TIC-TAC-TOE
Circle the words "eight."

eight	every	each
each	eight	eat
eat	every	eight

LETTER MAZE
Circle the letters that spell "eight."

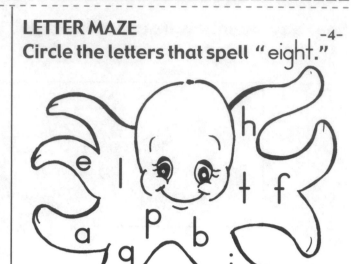

MISSING LETTERS: Fill in the missing letters for the word "eight."

e _____ t   __ i __ h __

e ____ h __   e __ g ____

COLORING WORDS:
Color each section that has the word "eight."

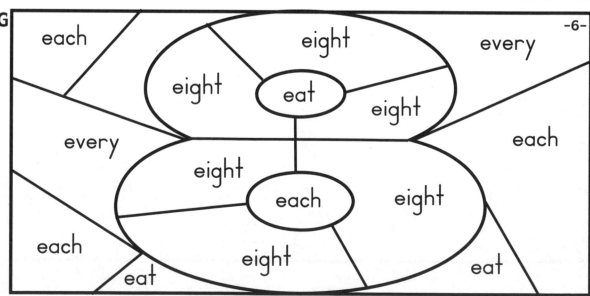

See. Say. Rainbow trace.

Cut and Paste.

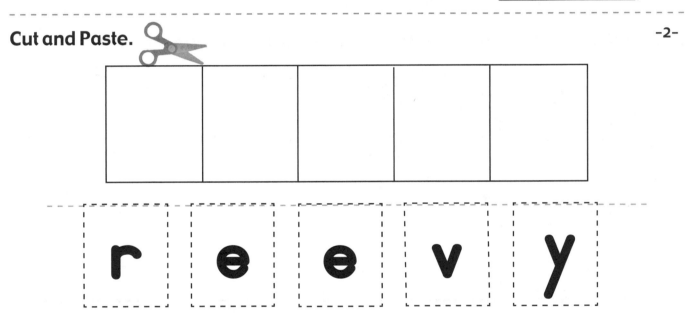

Trace and print.

every   every   every

_____   _____   _____

WORD SEARCH
Circle the words "every."

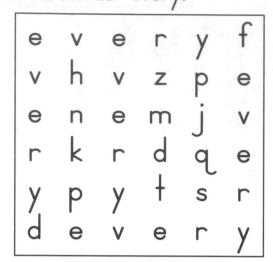

```
e v e r y f
v h v z p e
e n e m j v
r k r d q e
y p y t s r
d e v e r y
```

PYRAMID WORDS -4-
Build a pyramid for the word "every."

1. ___

2. ___ ___

3. ___ ___ ___

4. ___ ___ ___ ___

5. ___ ___ ___ ___ ___

(The first letter goes on the top line. The first and second letters go on the second line and so on.)

SCRAMBLED WORDS: Unscramble the letters to spell the word "every." -5-

eryve   eyevr   yeerv   ryeev

___ ___ ___ ___

COLORING WORDS: Color all of the birds that have the word "every." -6-

See. Say. Rainbow trace.

Cut and Paste.

d   n   f   i

Trace and print.

find   find   find   find

_____   _____   _____   _____

BLEND THE WORD
Draw a line to make the word "find."

WORD TIC-TAC-TOE
Circle the words "find."

-4-

five	four	five
four	dog	five
find	find	find

LETTER MAZE
Circle the letters that spell "find."

DOT-TO-DOT
Connect the letters that spell "find."

-5-

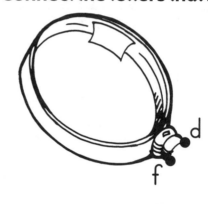

FINISH THE SENTENCE
Use the word "find" to fill in the blanks. Read each sentence.

-6-

1. Did you _____ the dog?

2. Can you _____ the cat?

3. I want to _____ a good book.

See. Say. Rainbow trace.

first

Cut and Paste.

t   f   s   r   i

Trace and print.

first   first   first

_____   _____   _____

WORD TIC-TAC-TOE
Circle the words "first."

four	find	first
five	five	first
four	find	first

LETTER MAZE
Circle the letters that spell "first."

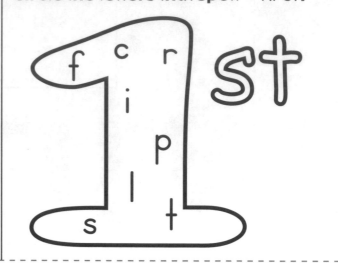

MISSING LETTERS: Fill in the missing letters for the word "first."

___ i ___ t

f ___ s ___

f ___ t

f ___ r ___

___ i ___ s ___

SPELL IT! Circle all of the words that spell "first."

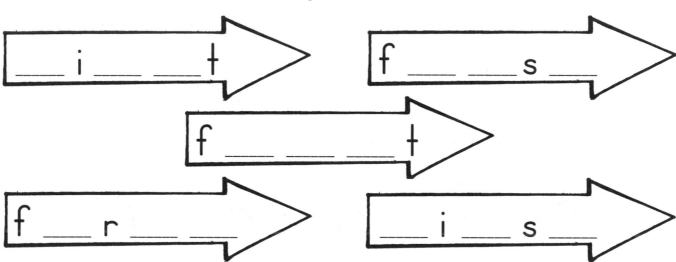

first place

first

find

first

five

first

first

find

first

five

See. Say. Rainbow trace.

Cut and Paste.

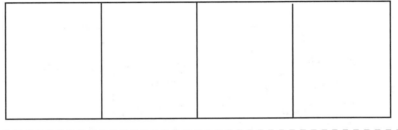

| v | e | f | i |

Trace and print.

five   five   five   five

_____   _____   _____   _____

WORD SEARCH
Circle the words "five."

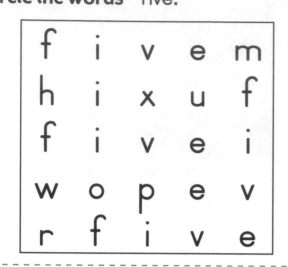

PYRAMID WORDS
-4-
Build a pyramid for the word "five."

1. ___f___

2. ___ ___

3. ___ ___ ___

4. ___ ___ ___ ___

(The first letter goes on the top line. The first and second letters go on the second line and so on.)

SCRAMBLED WORDS: Unscramble the letters to spell the word "five." -5-

 ifev

 fiev

 vfie

 fevi

_____   _____

COLORING WORDS: Color all of the 5's that have the word "five." -6-

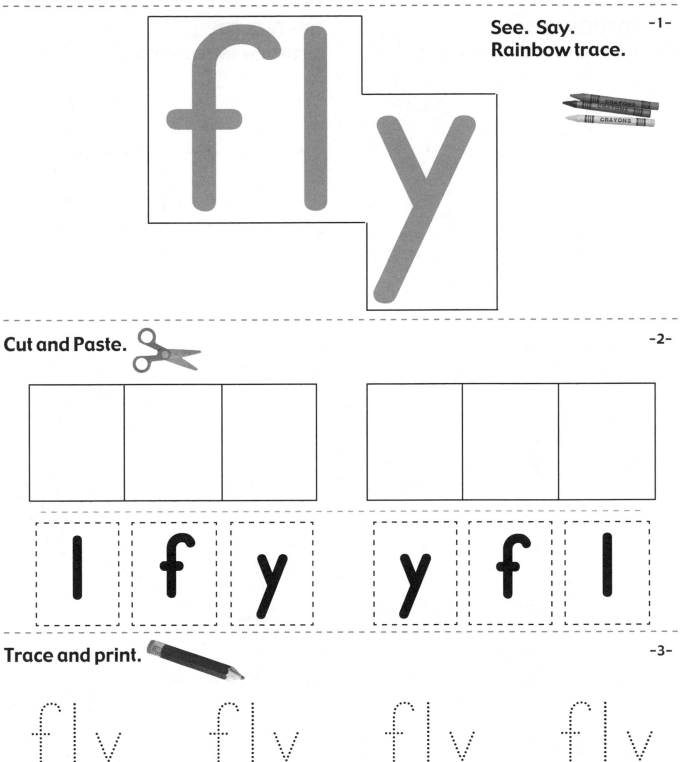

See. Say.
Rainbow trace. -1-

Cut and Paste. -2-

l	f	y

y	f	l

Trace and print. -3-

fly   fly   fly   fly

_____ _____ _____ _____

BLEND THE WORD
Draw a line to make the word "fly."

f   y

fl   ly

TIC-TAC-TOE
Circle the letters that spell "fly."

e	p	f
r	m	l
j	t	y

LETTER CONNECT
Connect the letters that spell "fly."

f   l   y

DOT-TO-DOT
Connect the letters that spell "fly."

f   l   y

FINISH THE SENTENCE:
Use the word "fly" to fill in the blanks. Read each sentence.

1. A bird can _____ .

2. She was going to _____ the plane.

3. Can a penguin _____ ?

See. Say. Rainbow trace.

Cut and Paste.

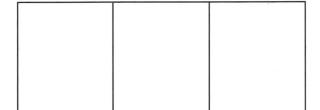

Trace and print.

for   for   for   for

_____   _____   _____   _____

TIC-TAC-TOE
Circle the letters that spell "for."

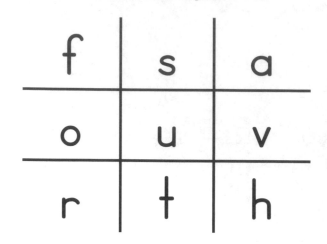

LETTER MAZE
Circle the letters that spell "for."

MISSING LETTERS: Fill in the missing letters for the word "for."

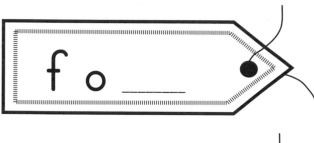

f o ___

___ ___ r

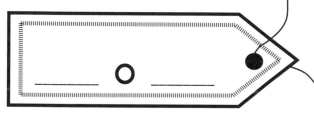

___ o ___

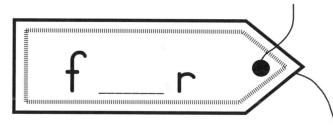

f ___ r

COLORING WORDS: Color all of the letters that have the word "for."

See. Say. Rainbow trace.

-1-

f**our**

Cut and Paste. ✂

-2-

o r f u

Trace and print. ✏

-3-

four four four

_____ _____ _____

WORD SEARCH
Circle the words "four."

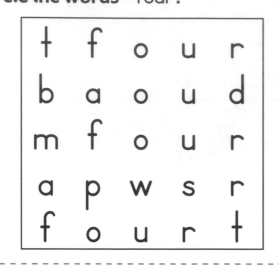

t f o u r
b a o u d
m f o u r
a p w s r
f o u r t

PYRAMID WORDS
Build a pyramid for the word "four."

1. ___f___

2. ___ ___

3. ___ ___ ___

4. ___ ___ ___ ___

(The first letter goes on the top line. The first and second letters go on the second line and so on.)

SCRAMBLED WORDS: Unscramble the letters to spell the word "four." −5−

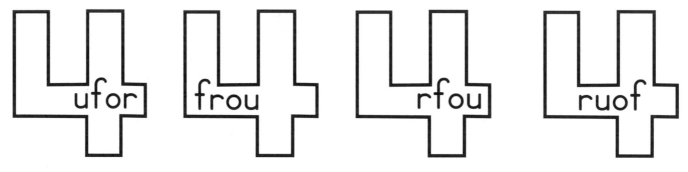

ufor   frou   rfou   ruof

___   ___   ___   ___

COLORING WORDS: Color all of the 4's that have the word "four." −6−

o   f   m   r

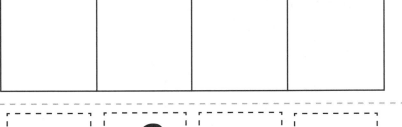

BLEND THE WORD
Draw a line to make the word "from."

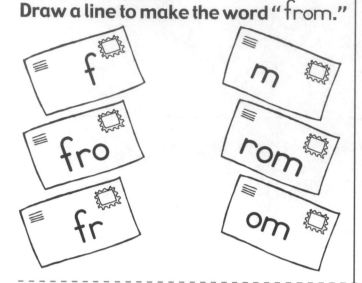

WORD TIC-TAC-TOE
Circle the words "from."

from	from	from
for	four	four
four	five	for

LETTER CONNECT
Connect the letters that spell "from."

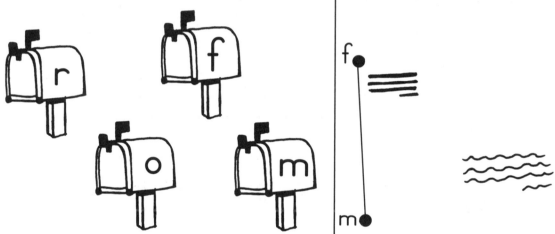

DOT-TO-DOT
Connect the letters that spell "from."

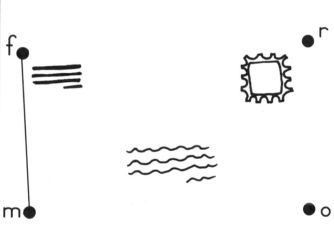

FINISH THE SENTENCE
Use the word "from" to fill in the blanks. Read each sentence.

1. Where are you _____ ?

2. The letter is _____ mom.

3. The dog came _____ the pet shop.

See. Say.
Rainbow trace.

Cut and Paste.

u   f   n   y   n

Trace and print.

funny   funny   funny

_____ _____ _____

WORD TIC-TAC-TOE
Circle the words "funny."

funny	five	four
from	funny	fun
fun	five	funny

LETTER MAZE
Circle the letters that spell "funny."

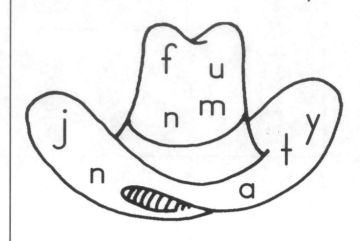

MISSING LETTERS: Fill in the missing letters for the word "funny."

___ u ___ ___ y   f ___ ___ ___ y

___ u ___ n ___   f ___ n ___ ___

SPELL IT! Circle all of the words that spell "funny."

See. Say. Rainbow trace.

Cut and Paste.

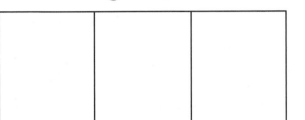

Trace and print.

get   get   get   get

_____   _____   _____   _____

WORD SEARCH
Circle the words "get."

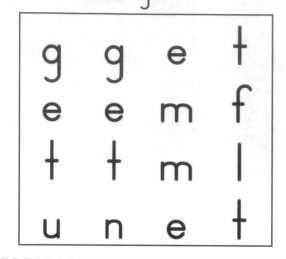

```
g  g  e  t
e  e  m  f
t  t  m  l
u  n  e  t
```

PYRAMID WORDS
Build a pyramid for the word "get." -4-

1. ___g___

2. ___ ___

3. ___ ___ ___

(The first letter goes on the top line. The first and second letters go on the second line and so on.)

SCRAMBLED WORDS: Unscramble the letters to spell the word "get." -5-

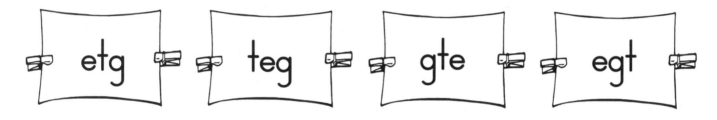

etg   teg   gte   egt

_____ _____ _____ _____

SPELL IT! Circle all of the words that spell "get." -6-

got   get   gut
   get
get   git   get   get

girl

Cut and Paste. -2-

r l i g

Trace and print. -3-

girl   girl   girl   girl

_____ _____ _____ _____ _____

BLEND THE WORD
Draw a line to make the word " girl."

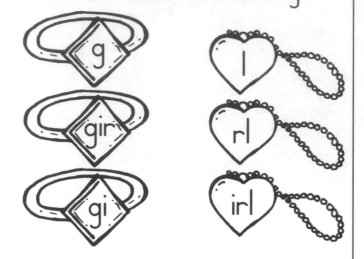

-4-

WORD TIC-TAC-TOE
Circle the words "girl."

get	girl	go
fly	girl	get
go	girl	fly

LETTER CONNECT
Connect the letters that spell "girl."

DOT-TO-DOT
Connect the letters that spell "girl."

-5-

FINISH THE SENTENCE

-6-

Use the word "girl" to fill in the blanks. Read each sentence.

1. There is a new _____ in class.

2. That _____ has a pet rabbit.

3. I am a friend of that _____ .

**See. Say.
Rainbow trace.**

give

Cut and Paste. ✂

v e i g

Trace and print.

give   give   give   give

_____ _____ _____ _____

WORD TIC-TAC-TOE
Circle the words "give."

girl	gave	get
get	girl	gave
give	give	give

PYRAMID WORDS
-4-
Build a pyramid for the word "give."

1. ___g___

2. ___ ___

3. ___ ___ ___

4. ___ ___ ___ ___

(The first letter goes on the top line. The first and second letters go on the second line and so on.)

MISSING LETTERS: Fill in the missing letters for the word "give."
-5-

g___ ___e   ___ i___ e   g i___ ___   g___ v___

SPELL IT! Circle all of the words that spell "give."
-6-

give   goes   give   get
gave   give   give   give
give   girl

See. Say. Rainbow trace.

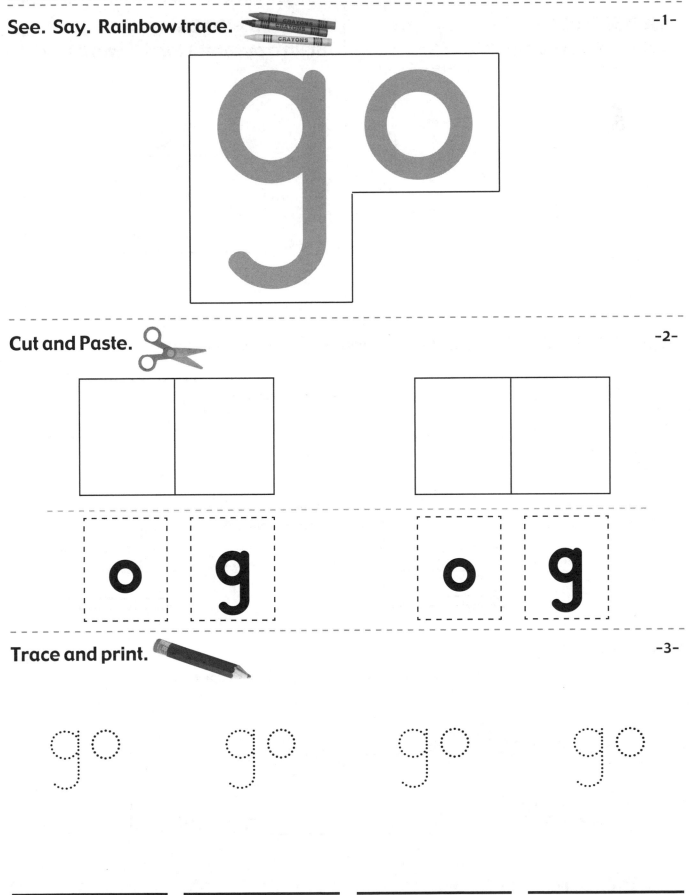

Cut and Paste.

o   g

o   g

Trace and print.

go   go   go   go

WORD SEARCH
Circle the words "go."

g	o	a	y
u	p	g	o
p	g	o	e
p	o	g	o

PYRAMID WORDS
Build a pyramid for the word "go."

1. ____g____

2. _____ _____

(The first letter goes on the top line. The first and second letters go on the second line and so on.)

MISSING LETTERS: Fill in the missing letters for the word "go." –5–

FINISH THE SENTENCE –6–
Use the word "go" to fill in the blanks. Read each sentence.

1. Where will we _____ ?

2. I want to _____ to school.

3. Did the dog _____ out?

See. Say. Rainbow trace. CRAYONS

good

Cut and Paste.

o   d   o   g

Trace and print.

good   good   good

_____   _____   _____

BLEND THE WORD
Draw a line to make the word "good."

WORD TIC-TAC-TOE
Circle the words "good."

get	give	good
give	go	good
go	get	good

LETTER CONNECT
Connect the letters that spell "good."

DOT-TO-DOT
Connect the letters that spell "good."

FINISH THE SENTENCE
Use the word "good" to fill in the blanks. Read each sentence.

1. I did _____ work in school.

2. She is _____ at math.

3. That is a _____ cat.

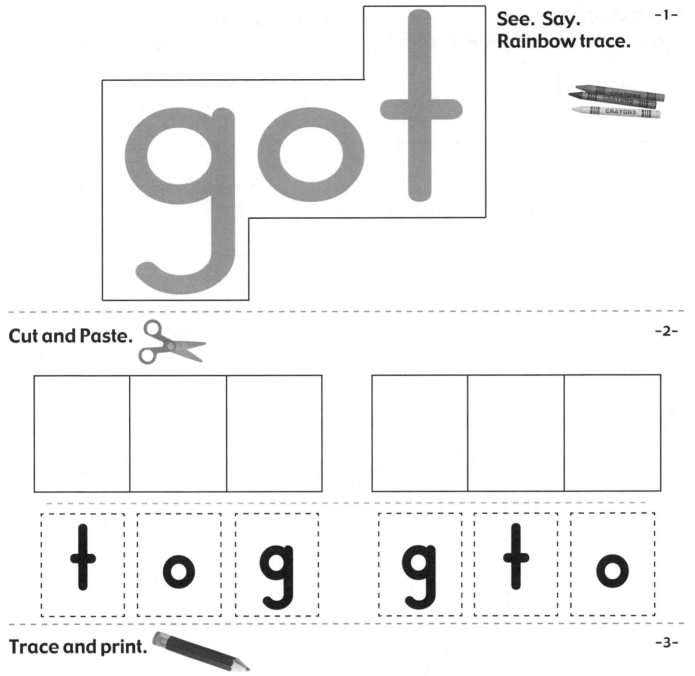

See. Say.
Rainbow trace.

got

Cut and Paste. ✂

| t | o | g | | g | t | o |

Trace and print. ✏

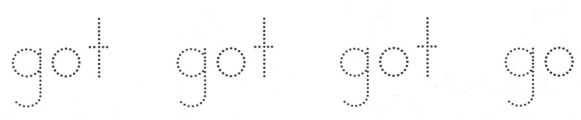

got   got   got   got

_____   _____   _____   _____

TIC-TAC-TOE
Circle the letters that spell "got."

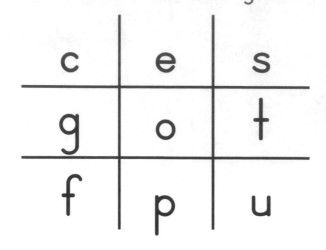

c	e	s
g	o	t
f	p	u

PYRAMID WORDS
Build a pyramid for the word "got." -4-

1. ___g___

2. ___ ___

3. ___ ___ ___

(The first letter goes on the top line. The first and second letters go on the second line and so on.)

MISSING LETTERS: Fill in the missing letters for the word "got." -5-

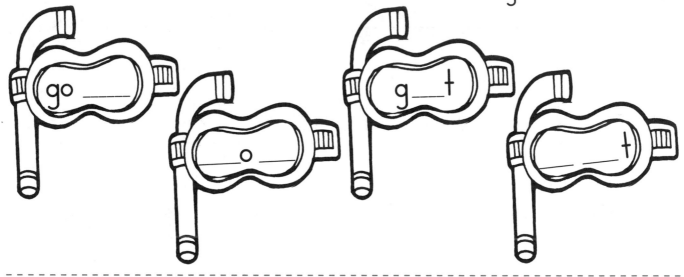

go___   ___o___   g___t   ___ ___ t

SPELL IT! Circle all of the words that spell "got." -6-

pot got got get got

lot got got got get

Cut and Paste. -2-

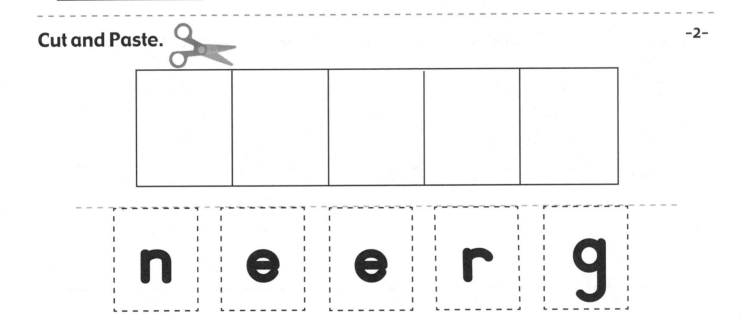

Trace and print. -3-

green   green   green

WORD SEARCH
Circle the words "green."

g	r	e	e	n	h
r	r	z	n	p	g
e	d	e	a	q	r
e	q	d	e	m	e
n	y	o	a	n	e
p	g	r	e	e	n

PYRAMID WORDS
-4-
Build a pyramid for the word "green."

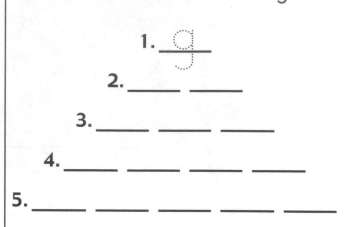

1. g
2. ___ ___
3. ___ ___ ___
4. ___ ___ ___ ___
5. ___ ___ ___ ___ ___

(The first letter goes on the top line. The first and second letters go on the second line and so on.)

SCRAMBLED WORDS: Unscramble the letters to spell the word "green." -5-

_____   _____   _____   _____

COLORING WORDS: Color all of the spots that have the word "green." -6-

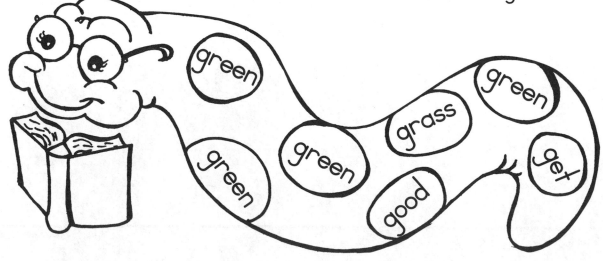

See. Say. Rainbow trace.

had

Cut and Paste.

d h a   a d h

Trace and print.

had   had   had   had

_____ _____ _____ _____

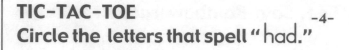

BLEND THE WORD
Draw a line to make the word "had."

TIC-TAC-TOE
-4-
Circle the letters that spell "had."

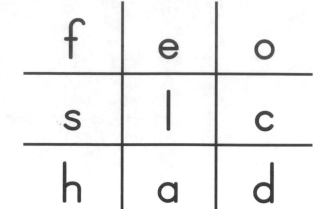

f	e	o
s	l	c
h	a	d

WORD MAZE
Circle all of the words that spell "had."

DOT-TO-DOT
-5-
Connect the letters that spell "had."

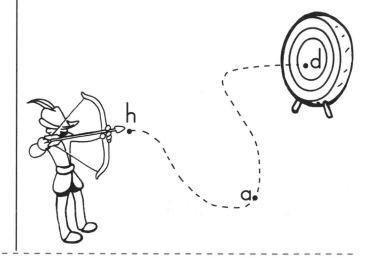

FINISH THE SENTENCE
-6-
Use the word "had" to fill in the blanks. Read each sentence.

1. I _____ a good lunch.

2. We _____ fun at school.

3. She _____ to help the teacher.

See. Say. Rainbow trace.

has

Cut and Paste. ✂

s a h a h s

Trace and print. ✏

has   has   has   has

_____   _____   _____   _____

TIC-TAC-TOE
Circle the letters that spell "has."

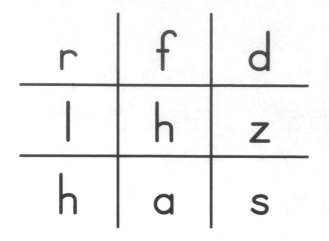

r	f	d
l	h	z
h	a	s

PYRAMID WORDS
-4-
Build a pyramid for the word "has."

1. ___h___

2. ___ ___

3. ___ ___ ___

(The first letter goes on the top line. The first and second letters go on the second line and so on.)

MISSING LETTERS: Fill in the missing letters for the word "has."
-5-

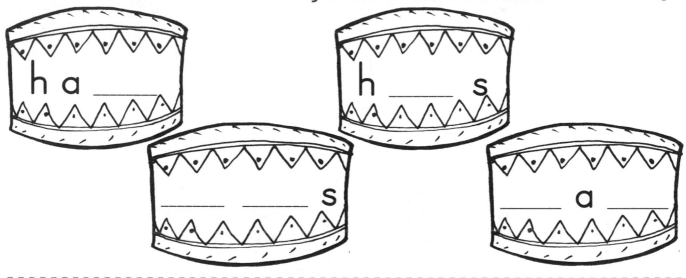

SPELL IT! Circle all of the words that spell "has."
-6-

See. Say. Rainbow trace.

Cut and Paste.

e   h   v   a

Trace and print. -3-

have   have   have

WORD SEARCH
Circle the words "have."

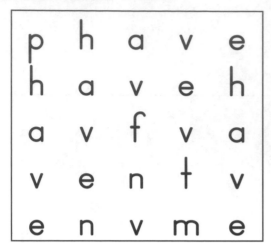

p	h	a	v	e
h	a	v	e	h
a	v	f	v	a
v	e	n	t	v
e	n	v	m	e

PYRAMID WORDS
Build a pyramid for the word "have." — -4-

1. __h____

2. ____ ____

3. ____ ____ ____

4. ____ ____ ____ ____

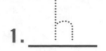

(The first letter goes on the top line. The first and second letters go on the second line and so on.)

SCRAMBLED WORDS: Unscramble the letters to spell the word "have." — -5-

heva

avhe

ehva

vaeh

_____   _____   _____   _____

COLORING WORDS: Color all of the flowers that have the word "have." — -6-

have   hand   have   has

have   here   hold   have

See. Say. Rainbow trace.

he

Cut and Paste.

e	h

e	h

Trace and print.

he   he   he   he

_____   _____   ____   _____

PYRAMID WORDS
Build a pyramid for the word "he."

1. ___h___

2. _____ _____

(The first letter goes on the top line. The first and second letters go on the second line and so on.)

WORD TIC-TAC-TOE
Circle the words "he."

he	has	her
her	he	here
here	has	he

WORD MAZE
Circle the words that spell "he."

he
hi he
ha ho
he he

hi
ho he
he
ha he

DOT-TO-DOT
Connect the letters that spell "he."

h•   •e

h•   •e

FINISH THE SENTENCE
Use the word "he" to fill in the blanks. Read each sentence.

1. I think _____ is nice.

2. Can _____ play at my house?

3. Look, _____ can run fast!

Cut and Paste.  -2-

e h l p

Trace and print.  -3-

help   help   help   help

_____   _____   _____   _____

WORD TIC-TAC-TOE
Circle the words "help."

help	here	held
help	had	here
help	here	hold

LETTER MAZE
Circle the letters that spell "help."

h d e
l
g a p

MISSING LETTERS: Fill in the missing letters for the word "help."

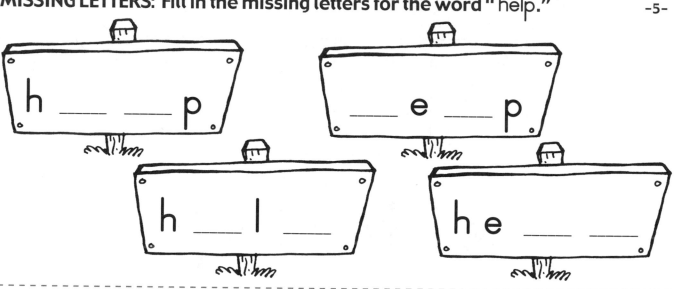

h ___ ___ p

___ e ___ p

h ___ l ___

h e ___ ___

SPELL IT! Circle all of the words that spell "help."

help   help

help   here
have
held   help

help   heep
help

help

Cut and Paste. ✂ -2-

r e h e h r

Trace and print. -3-

her her her her

_____ _____ _____ _____

WORD SEARCH
Circle the words "her."

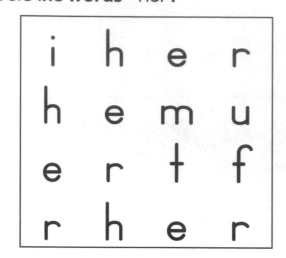

i	h	e	r
h	e	m	u
e	r	t	f
r	h	e	r

PYRAMID WORDS   -4-
Build a pyramid for the word "her."

1. ___h___

2. _____ _____

3. _____ _____ _____

(The first letter goes on the top line. The first and second letters go on the second line and so on.)

SCRAMBLED WORDS: Unscramble the letters to spell the word "her."   -5-

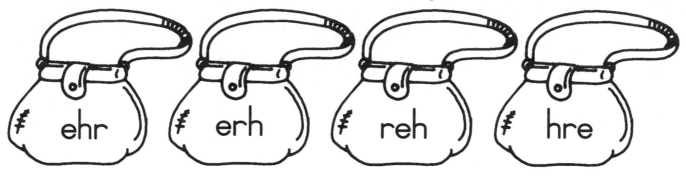

ehr   erh   reh   hre

_____ _____ _____ _____

COLORING WORDS: Color all of the stars that have the word "her."   -6-

her   her   here   her

hers   her   he   her

See. Say. Rainbow trace.

Cut and Paste.

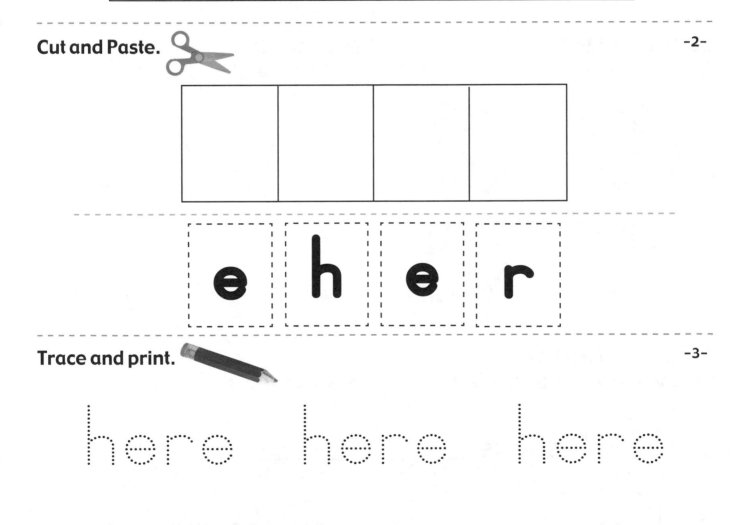

e h e r

Trace and print. -3-

here here here

BLEND THE WORD
Draw a line to make the word "here."

h

he

her

e

ere

re

help	her	he
here	here	here
he	help	her

LETTER CONNECT
Connect the letters that spell "here."

r

e

e

h

e

r

e

h

FINISH THE SENTENCE —6—
Use the word "here" to fill in the blanks. Read each sentence.

1. I think she is _____ .

2. Look, _____ are the crayons.

3. He is going to be _____ .

See. Say. Rainbow trace.

him

Cut and Paste.

m   i   h   i   h   m

Trace and print.

him   him   him   him

_____ _____ _____ _____

TIC-TAC-TOE
Circle the letters that spell "him."

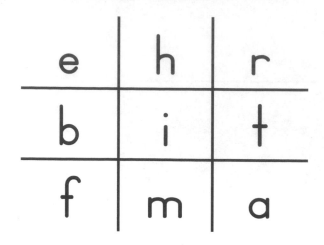

e	h	r
b	i	t
f	m	a

PYRAMID WORDS
Build a pyramid for the word "him." -4-

1. __h__

2. ___ ___

3. ___ ___ ___

(The first letter goes on the top line. The first and second letters go on the second line and so on.)

MISSING LETTERS: Fill in the missing letters for the word "him." -5-

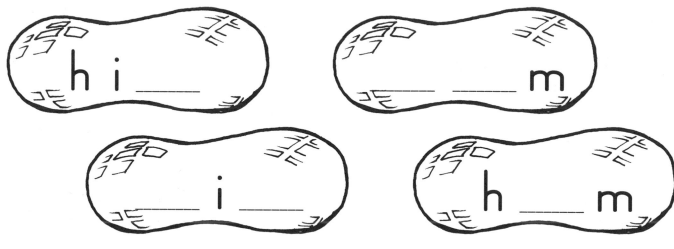

h i ___   ___ ___ m

___ i ___   h ___ m

COLORING WORDS
Color all of the elephant ears that have the word "him."

-6-

had — him   him — hit

him — his   him — her   his — him

See. Say. Rainbow trace. -1-

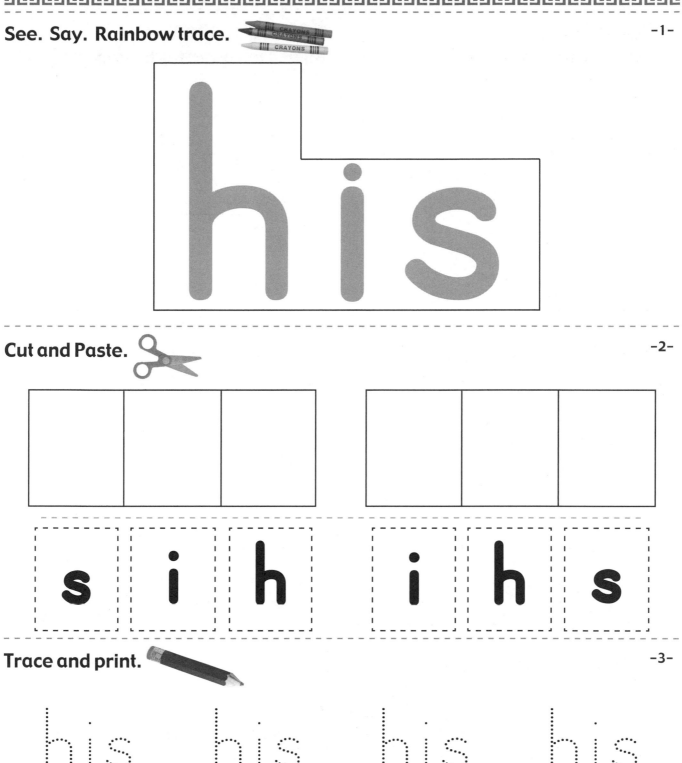

Cut and Paste. -2-

s   i   h   i   h   s

Trace and print. -3-

his   his   his   his

_____ _____ _____ _____

WORD SEARCH
Circle the words "his."

h	i	s	m
z	h	o	h
s	a	i	i
u	h	i	s

PYRAMID WORDS
Build a pyramid for the word "his." -4-

1. __h__

2. _____ _____

3. _____ _____ _____

(The first letter goes on the top line. The first and second letters go on the second line and so on.)

SCRAMBLED WORDS: Unscramble the letters to spell the word "his." -5-

ish
_____

shi
_____

sih
_____

hsi
_____

COLORING WORDS: Color all of the bananas that have the word "his." -6-

Cut and Paste. ✂ -2-

┌╌╌╌┐ ┌╌╌╌┐ ┌╌╌╌┐ ┌╌╌╌┐ ┌╌╌╌┐
┆ u ┆ ┆ h ┆ ┆ s ┆ ┆ e ┆ ┆ o ┆
└╌╌╌┘ └╌╌╌┘ └╌╌╌┘ └╌╌╌┘ └╌╌╌┘

Trace and print. ✏ -3-

house   house   house

_____   _____   _____

BLEND THE WORD
Draw a line to make the word "house."

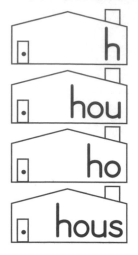
h

hou

ho

hous

e

use

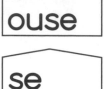
ouse

se

WORD TIC-TAC-TOE
Circle the words "house."

had	house	help
have	house	had
help	house	have

LETTER CONNECT
Connect the letters that spell "house."

DOT-TO-DOT
Connect the letters that spell "house."

FINISH THE SENTENCE
Use the word "house" to fill in the blanks. Read each sentence.

1. This is a new _____ .

2. Let's play at my _____ .

3. I like that _____ .

how

w　o　h　　o　h　w

how　how　how　how

_____　_____　_____　_____

TIC-TAC-TOE
Circle the letters that spell "how."

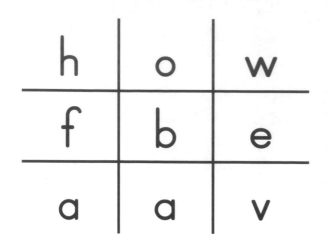

PYRAMID WORDS
Build a pyramid for the word "how."
-4-

1. h _____

2. _____ _____

3. _____ _____ _____

(The first letter goes on the top line. The first and second letters go on the second line and so on.)

MISSING LETTERS: Fill in the missing letters for the word "how." —5—

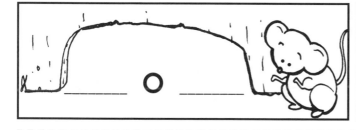

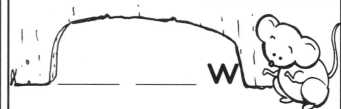

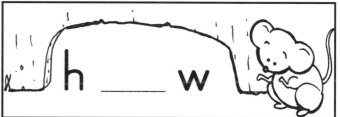

SPELL IT! Circle all of the words that spell "how." —6—

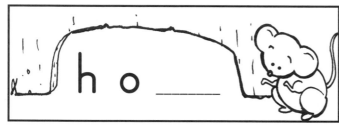

See. Say. Rainbow trace.

I   I   I

Cut and Paste. ✂

_____ like 🍦 .

_____ like 🧀 .

_____ like 🍒 .

_____ like 🍕 .

I   I

I   I

Trace and print. ✏

I   I   I   I   I

_____ _____ _____ _____ _____ _____

TIC-TAC-TOE
Circle all of the "I" letters.

I	t	f
t	I	t
f	f	I

LETTER MAZE
Color every letter "I" in the ice cube tray.

-4-

I	I	t	I
f	I	J	I

COLOR THE LETTERS
Decorate each letter "I."

-5-

I I I

FINISH THE SENTENCE
Use the word "I" to fill in the blanks. Read each sentence. Draw a picture.

-6-

1. _____ see a dog.

2. _____ like you.

See. Say. Rainbow trace.

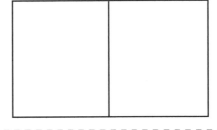

Cut and Paste.

Trace and print.

if   if   if   if

——————— ——————— ——————— ———————

MISSING LETTERS
Fill in the missing letters for the word "if."

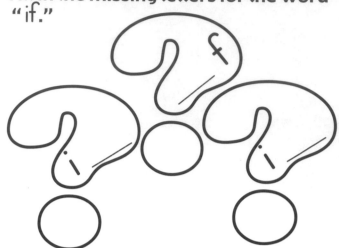

if	it	in
is	if	in
in	is	if

PYRAMID WORDS
Build a pyramid for the word "if."

1. _____

2. _____ _____

(The first letter goes on the top line. The first and second letters go on the second line and so on.)

COLORING WORDS: Color all of the shoes that have the word "if."

See. Say. Rainbow trace.

Cut and Paste.

n   i   n   i

Trace and print.

in   in   in   in

WORD TIC-TAC-TOE
Circle the words "in."

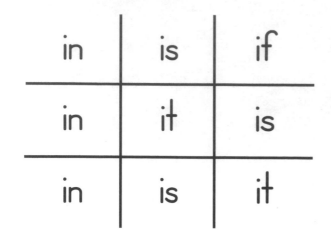

in	is	if
in	it	is
in	is	it

WORD MAZE
Circle all the words that spell "in."

in   it   is
in   is   in   is
       if   in   in

MISSING LETTERS: Fill in the missing letters for the word "in."

___ n   i ___   i ___   ___ n

COLORING WORDS: Color all of the birds that have the word "in."

is   in   in   if

in   on   it   in

See. Say. Rainbow trace.

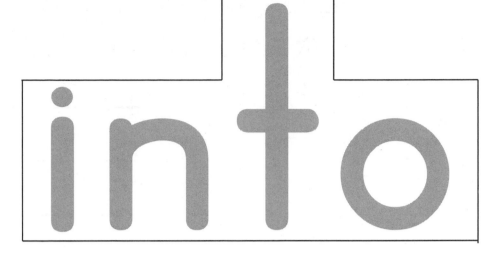

Cut and Paste.

Trace and print.

into   into   into   into

_____ _____ _____ _____

WORD SEARCH
Circle the words "into."

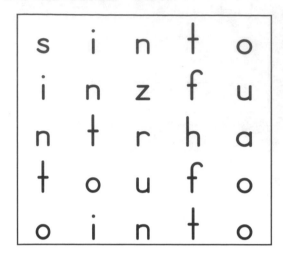

s	i	n	t	o
i	n	z	f	u
n	t	r	h	a
t	o	u	f	o
o	i	n	t	o

PYRAMID WORDS
-4-
Build a pyramid for the word "into."

1. ___
2. ___ ___
3. ___ ___ ___
4. ___ ___ ___ ___

(The first letter goes on the top line. The first and second letters go on the second line and so on.)

SCRAMBLED WORDS: Unscramble the letters to spell the word "into."   -5-

toin   iton   oint   onti

_____   _____   _____   _____

SPELL IT! Circle all of the words that spell "into."   -6-

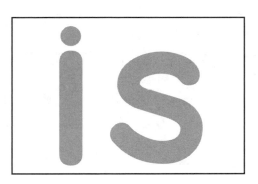

Cut and Paste. ✂

-2-

s i   s i

Trace and print. ✏

-3-

is   is   is   is

_____ _____ _____ _____

MISSING LETTERS
Fill in the missing letters for the word "is."

WORD TIC-TAC-TOE
Circle the words " is."

is	as	in
is	it	as
is	in	if

LETTER CONNECT
Connect the letters that spell " is" twice.

PYRAMID WORDS
Build a pyramid for the word " is."

1. _____

2. _____ _____

(The first letter goes on the top line. The first and second letters go on the second line and so on.)

FINISH THE SENTENCE
Use the word " is" to fill in the blanks. Read each sentence.

1. She _____ going to school.

2. Where _____ he going?

3. How _____ he feeling?

See. Say. Rainbow trace.

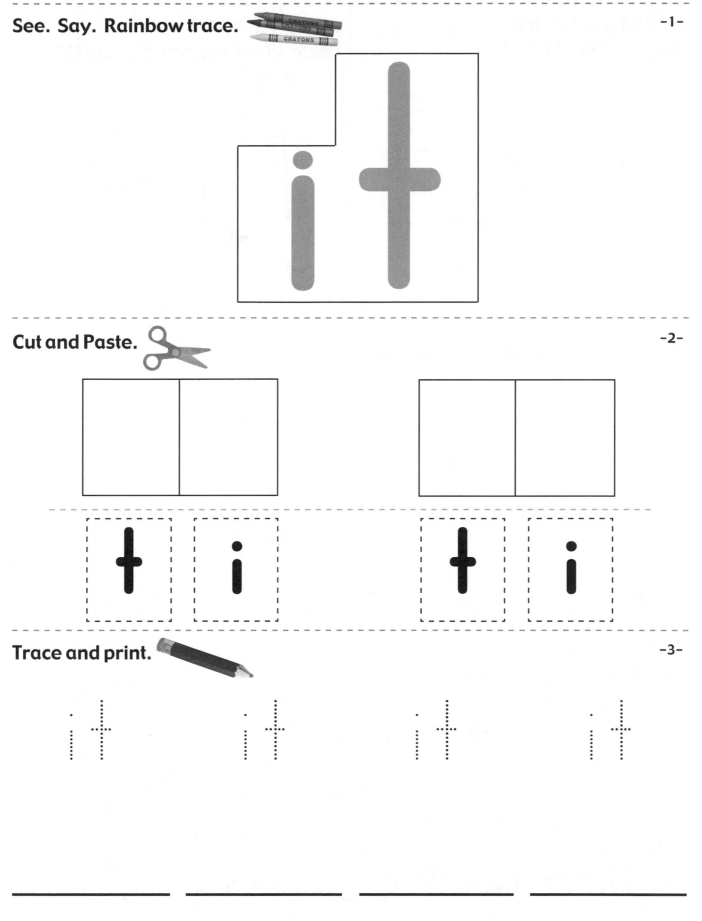

Cut and Paste.

Trace and print.

WORD TIC-TAC-TOE
Circle the words "it."

it	is	if
is	it	in
if	in	it

WORD MAZE
Circle all of the words that spell "it."

MISSING LETTERS: Fill in the missing letters for the word "it."

i ___   ___ t   ___ t   i ___

COLORING WORDS
Color all of the apples that have the word "it."

See. Say. Rainbow trace.

its

Cut and Paste.

i s t   t s i

Trace and print.

its   its   its   its

_____ _____ _____ _____

WORD SEARCH
Circle the words "its."

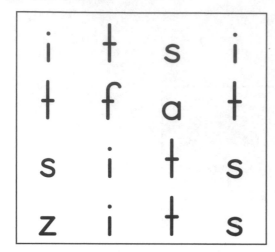

```
i  t  s  s  i
t  f  a  t
s  i  t  s
z  z  i  t  s
```

PYRAMID WORDS
Build a pyramid for the word "its." -4-

1. ___i___

2. _____ _____

3. _____ _____ _____

(The first letter goes on the top line. The first and second letters go on the second line and so on.)

SCRAMBLED WORDS: Unscramble the letters to spell the word "its." -5-

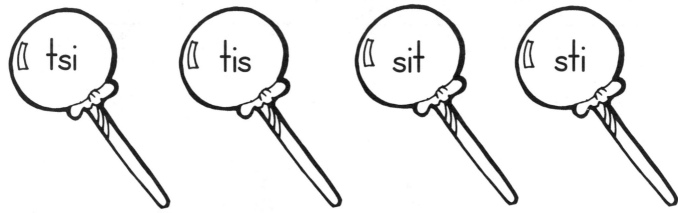

tsi   tis   sit   sti

_____   _____   _____   _____

COLORING WORDS: Color all of the candies that have the word "its." -6-

Cut and Paste. 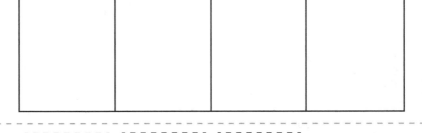 -2-

Trace and print. -3-

j u m p   j u m p   j u m p

WORD TIC-TAC-TOE
Circle the words "jump."

jam	just	like
just	like	jam
jump	jump	jump

LETTER MAZE
Circle the letters that spell "jump."

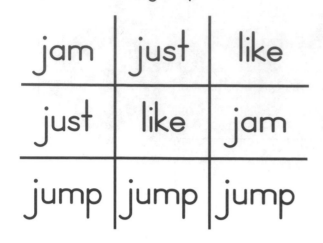

a p

g

m b

t

j y c u

MISSING LETTERS: Fill in the missing letters for the word "jump."

j ___ ___ p

___ u ___ p

j u ___ ___

j ___ m ___

SPELL IT! Circle all of the words that spell "jump."

just

jump

funny

jump

jump

give

jump

give

just

jump

just

jump

give

jump

funny

See. Say. Rainbow trace.

just

Cut and Paste.

s   t   u   j

Trace and print.

just   just   just

WORD SEARCH
Circle the words "just."

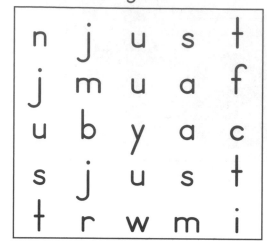

n	j	u	s	t
j	m	u	a	f
u	b	y	a	c
s	j	u	s	t
t	r	w	m	i

PYRAMID WORDS
-4-
Build a pyramid for the word "just."

1. ___

2. ___ ___

3. ___ ___ ___

4. ___ ___ ___ ___

(The first letter goes on the top line. The first and second letters go on the second line and so on.)

SCRAMBLED WORDS: Unscramble the letters to spell the word "just."   -5-

usjt   stju   tjus   jstu

___   ___   ___   ___

COLORING WORDS
Color all of the circles that have the word "just."

-6-

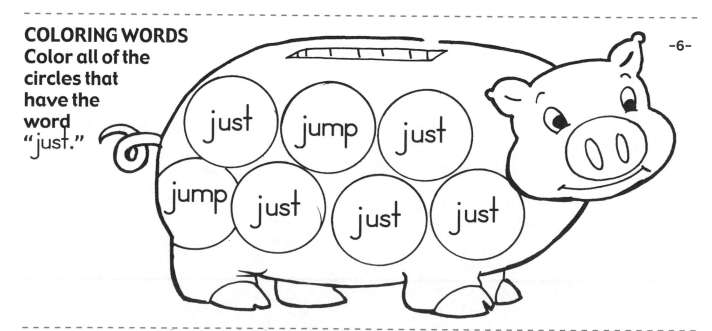

just   jump   just
jump   just   just   just

See. Say. Rainbow trace.

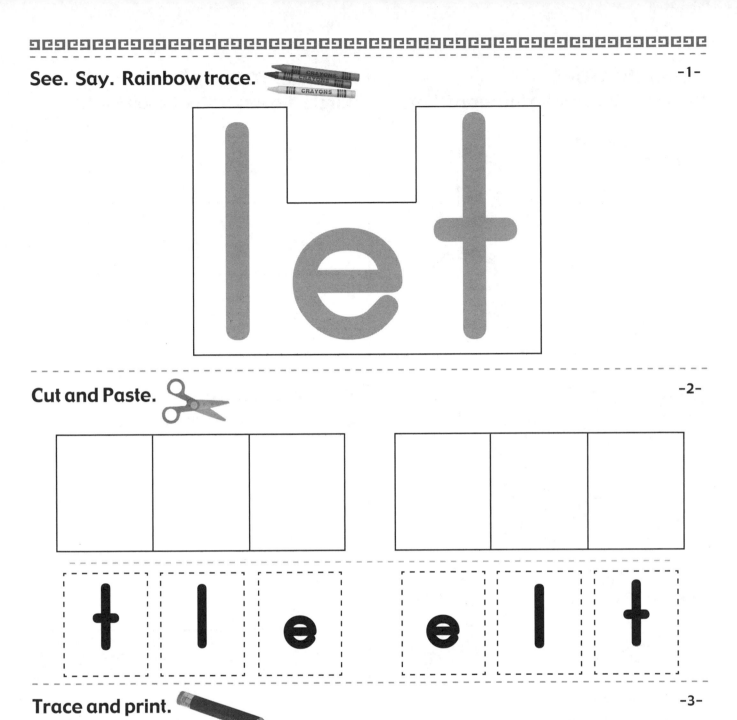

Cut and Paste.

Trace and print.

let   let   let   let

BLEND THE WORD
Draw a line to make the word "let."

le

et

l

t

TIC-TAC-TOE
-4-
Circle the letters that spell "let."

l	g	h
m	e	a
y	u	t

LETTER CONNECT
Connect the letters that spell "let."

l

e

t

PYRAMID WORDS
-5-
Build a pyramid for the word "let."

1. _____

2. _____ _____

3. _____ _____ _____

(The first letter goes on the top line. The first and second letters go on the second line and so on.)

FINISH THE SENTENCE
-6-
Use the word "let" to fill in the blanks. Read each sentence.

1. I _____ the dog in the house.

2. Will you _____ me help?

3. I _____ the boy play with my toy.

See. Say. Rainbow trace.

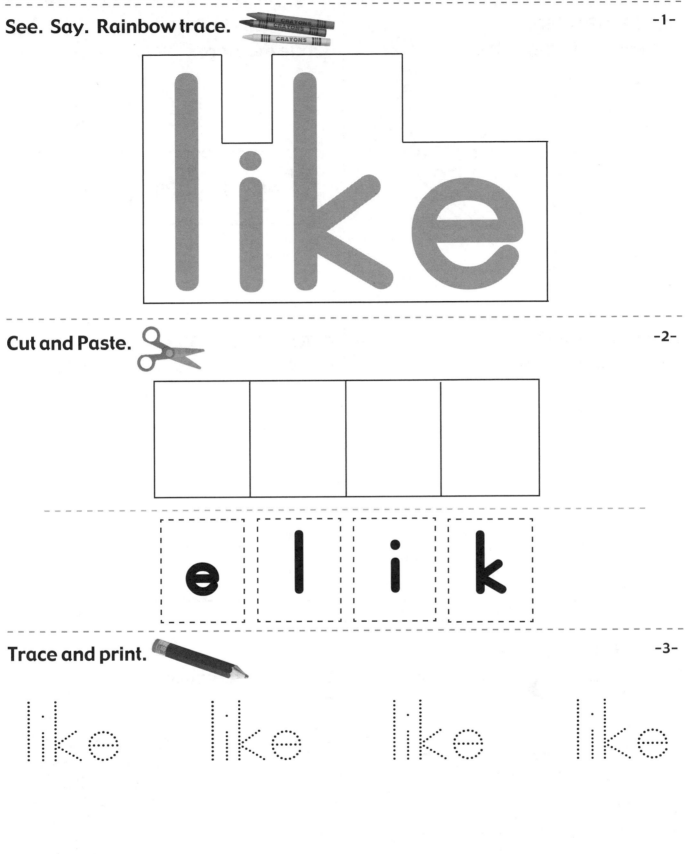

Cut and Paste.

e   l   i   k

Trace and print.

like   like   like   like

_____   _____   _____   _____

BLEND THE WORD
Draw a line to make the word "like."

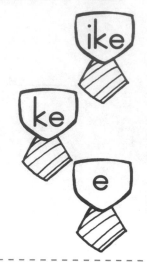

WORD TIC-TAC-TOE
Circle the words "like."

its	look	into
like	like	like
into	its	look

LETTER CONNECT
Connect the letters that spell "like."

PYRAMID WORDS
Build a pyramid for the word "like."

1. ____

2. ____ ____

3. ____ ____ ____

4. ____ ____ ____ ____

(The first letter goes on the top line. The first and second letters go on the second line and so on.)

FINISH THE SENTENCE
Use the word "like" to fill in the blanks. Read each sentence.

1. I _____ to run.

2. Do you _____ me?

3. I would _____ to eat a cookie.

See. Say. Rainbow trace.

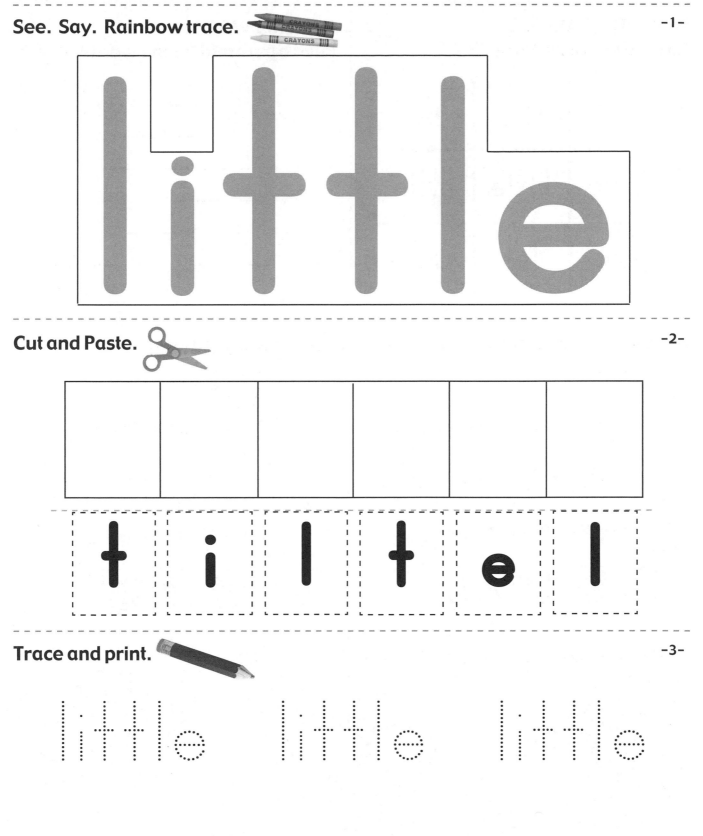

Cut and Paste.

Trace and print.

WORD TIC-TAC-TOE
Circle the words "little."

just	like	let
little	little	little
like	let	jump

PYRAMID WORDS
Build a pyramid for the word "little."

-4-

1. ____
2. ____ ____
3. ____ ____ ____
4. ____ ____ ____ ____
5. ____ ____ ____ ____ ____
6. ____ ____ ____ ____ ____ ____

(The first letter goes on the top line. The first and second letters go on the second line and so on.)

MISSING LETTERS: Fill in the missing letters for the word "little." -5-

__ i __ __ l e

l __ __ __ t l __

l __ __ __ l e

l __ t __ l __

SPELL IT! Color each butterfly that has the word "little." -6-

**See. Say.
Rainbow trace.**

long

Cut and Paste.

o l n g

Trace and print.

long   long   long   long

_____   _____   _____   _____

WORD SEARCH
Circle the words "long."

l	l	o	n	g
o	m	l	r	c
n	l	o	n	g
g	z	n	s	w
e	p	g	u	k

PYRAMID WORDS
-4-
Build a pyramid for the word "long."

1. _____

2. _____ _____

3. _____ _____ _____

4. _____ _____ _____ _____

(The first letter goes on the top line. The first and second letters go on the second line and so on.)

SCRAMBLED WORDS: Unscramble the letters to spell the word "long." -5-

gnol   onlg   lgon   nglo

_____ _____ _____ _____

COLORING WORDS: Color all of the tags that have the word "long." -6-

Cut and Paste. -2-

Trace and print. -3-

look   look   look   look

_____ _____ _____ _____

BLEND THE WORD
Draw a line to make the word "look."

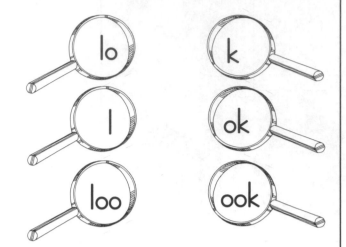

WORD TIC-TAC-TOE
Circle the words "look."

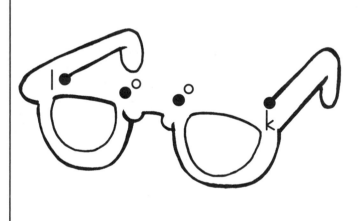

little	look	like
like	look	let
let	look	little

LETTER CONNECT
Connect the letters that spell "look."

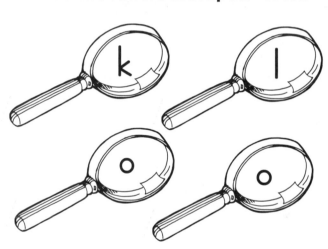

DOT-TO-DOT
Connect the letters that spell "look."

FINISH THE SENTENCE
Use the word "look" to fill in the blanks. Read each sentence.

1. Go and _____ for the cat.

2. I can _____ for the book.

3. Did you _____ for the dog?

made

d m a e

made   made   made

_____   _____   _____

WORD TIC-TAC-TOE
Circle the words "made."

made	mom	mom
moon	made	make
make	more	made

LETTER MAZE
Circle the letters that spell "made."

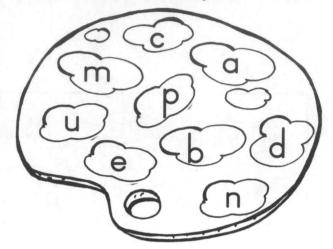

MISSING LETTERS: Fill in the missing letters for the word "made."

m ___ ___ e

___ a ___ e

m ___ d ___

m a ___ ___

COLORING WORDS: Color all of the ovals that have the word "made."

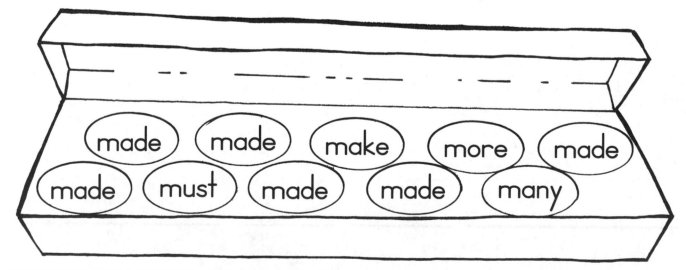

made   made   make   more   made

made   must   made   made   many

Cut and Paste. -2-

k   a   m   e

Trace and print. -3-

make   make   make

_____   _____   _____

WORD SEARCH
Circle the words "make."

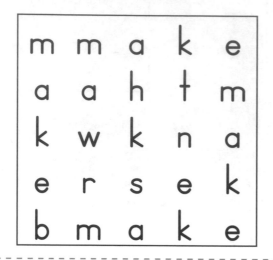

m	m	a	k	e
a	a	h	t	m
k	w	k	n	a
e	r	s	e	k
b	m	a	k	e

PYRAMID WORDS
Build a pyramid for the word "make."

1. ___m___

2. ___ ___

3. ___ ___ ___

4. ___ ___ ___ ___

(The first letter goes on the top line. The first and second letters go on the second line and so on.)

SCRAMBLED WORDS: Unscramble the letters to spell the word "make."

 kmae

 kema

 amek

 mkae

_____   _____   _____   _____

SPELL IT! Circle all of the words that spell "make."

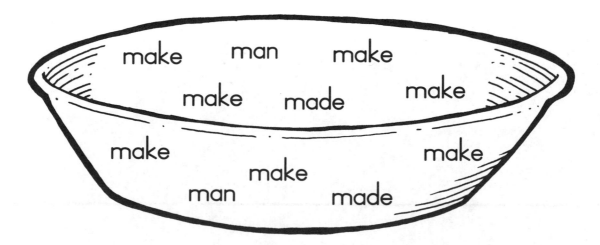

make   man   make
make   made   make
make   make
make   man   made

See. Say. Rainbow trace.

many

Cut and Paste. ✂

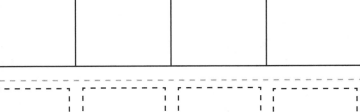

y a m n

Trace and print. ✏

many   many   many

BLEND THE WORD
Draw a line to make the word "many."

m

ma

man

ny

any

y

WORD TIC-TAC-TOE
Circle the words "many."

many	many	many
made	make	more
make	more	made

LETTER MAZE
Circle the letters that spell "many."

w   n

m   y   g

a   u

c

DOT-TO-DOT
Connect the letters that spell "many."

y

m

n

a

FINISH THE SENTENCE
Use the word "many" to fill in the blanks. Read each sentence.

1. How _____ cookies do you want?

2. There are _____ birds.

3. My mom has _____ friends.

See. Say. Rainbow trace.

may

Cut and Paste.

a	m	y

y	a	m

Trace and print.

may   may   may   may

_____   _____

TIC-TAC-TOE
Circle the letters that spell "may."

LETTER MAZE
Circle the letters that spell "may."

y	e	p
m	a	y
g	o	n

MISSING LETTERS: Fill in the missing letters for the word "may."

m a ____

____ a ____

____ ____ y

m ____ y

SPELL IT! Circle all of the words that spell "may."

may   my   man   may   man   may   may   my

Cut and Paste. ✂ -2-

e m   e m

Trace and print. ✏ -3-

me   me   me   me

_____   _____   _____   _____

WORD SEARCH
Circle the words "me."

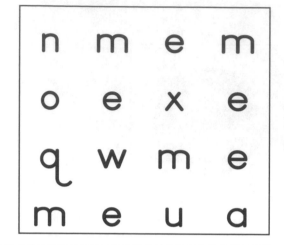

n	m	e	m
o	e	x	e
q	w	m	e
m	e	u	a

PYRAMID WORDS
Build a pyramid for the word "me."

−4−

1. ___m___

2. _____ _____

(The first letter goes on the top line. The first and second letters go on the second line and so on.)

MISSING LETTERS: Fill in the missing letters for the word "me."

−5−

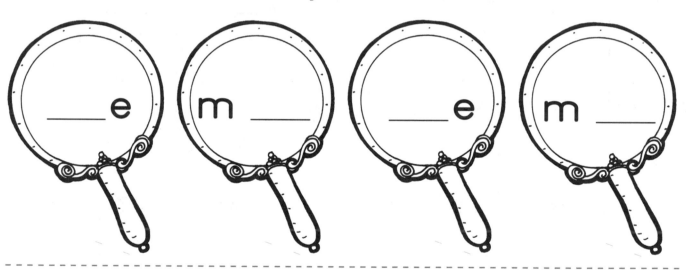

__e   m__   __e   m__

SPELL IT! Circle all of the words that spell "me."

−6−

me	my	me	me
men	my	men	
me	me	my	me

mom

Cut and Paste. -2-

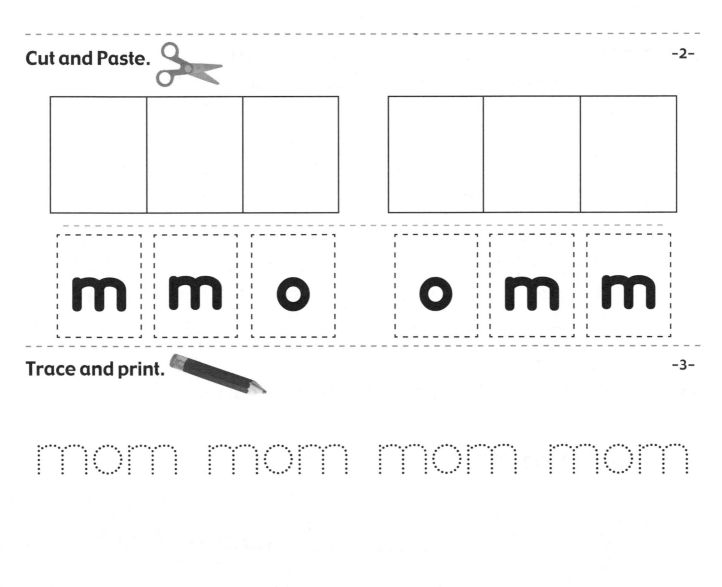

m   m   o   o   m   m

Trace and print. -3-

mom mom mom mom

_____ _____ _____ _____

BLEND THE WORD
Draw a line to make the word "mom."

TIC-TAC-TOE
-4-
Circle the letters that spell "mom."

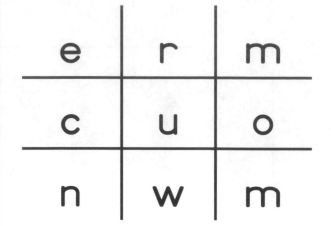

LETTER CONNECT
Connect the letters that spell "mom."

DOT-TO-DOT
-5-
Connect the letters that spell "mom."

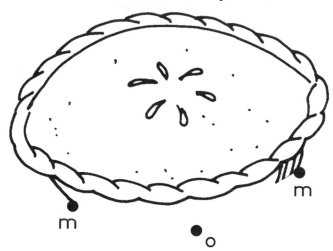

FINISH THE SENTENCE
-6-
Use the word "mom" to fill in the blanks. Read each sentence.

1. She is my _____ .

2. My _____ will make us lunch.

3. I have the best _____ .

Cut and Paste. ✂ -2-

s m t u

Trace and print. ✏ -3-

must must must

_____ _____ _____

WORD TIC-TAC-TOE
Circle the words "must."

must	many	make
must	make	many
must	made	made

PYRAMID WORDS
Build a pyramid for the word "must."

1. _m_

2. ___ ___

3. ___ ___ ___

4. ___ ___ ___ ___

(The first letter goes on the top line. The first and second letters go on the second line and so on.)

MISSING LETTERS: Fill in the missing letters for the word "must."

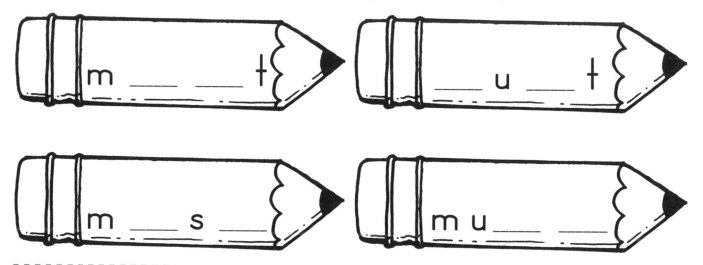

m ___ ___ t

___ u ___ t

m ___ s ___

m u ___ ___

SPELL IT! Circle all of the words that spell "must."

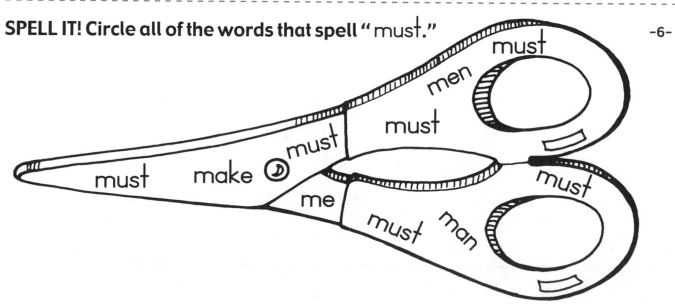

must   men   must   me   must   man   make   must   must

See. Say. Rainbow trace.

my

Cut and Paste.

y m   y m

Trace and print.

my   my   my   my

_____ _____ _____ _____

WORD SEARCH
Circle the words "my."

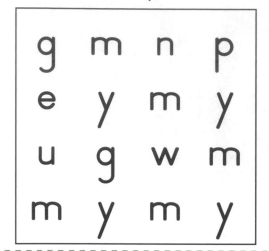

g m n p
e y m y
u g w m
m y m y

PYRAMID WORDS
-4-
Build a pyramid for the word "my."

1. ____m____

2. _____ _____

(The first letter goes on the top line. The first and second letters go on the second line and so on.)

MISSING LETTERS: Fill in the missing letters for the word "my." -5-

m____   ____y   ____y   m____

COLORING WORDS: Color all of the shoes that have the word "my." -6-

my me   no my   my up

up my   me my

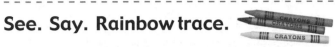

Cut and Paste. ✂ -2-

w	e	n

n	w	e

Trace and print. ✏ -3-

new   new   new   new

_____   _____   _____   _____

BLEND THE WORD
Draw a line to make the word "new."

n

w

ne

ew

TIC-TAC-TOE
Circle the letters that spell "new."

o	u	m
n	e	w
z	a	o

LETTER CONNECT
Connect the letters that spell "new."

w

e

n

DOT-TO-DOT
Connect the letters that spell "new."

e

w

n

FINISH THE SENTENCE
Use the word "new" to fill in the blanks. Read each sentence.

1. I have a _____ cat.

2. Do you like my _____ hat?

3. That is my _____ teacher.

See. Say. Rainbow trace.

nine.

Cut and Paste. ✂

n n i e

Trace and print. ✏

nine   nine   nine   nine

_____ _____ _____ _____

WORD TIC-TAC-TOE
Circle the words "nine."

many	nine	now
no	nine	new
new	nine	many

PYRAMID WORDS
Build a pyramid for the word "nine."

-4-

1. _n_

2. ___ ___

3. ___ ___ ___

4. ___ ___ ___ ___

(The first letter goes on the top line. The first and second letters go on the second line and so on.)

MISSING LETTERS: Fill in the missing letters for the word "nine."
-5-

9. ___ i ___ e

 **9.** n ___ ___ e

9. n ___ n ___

9. n i ___ ___

SPELL IT! Circle all of the words that spell "nine."
-6-

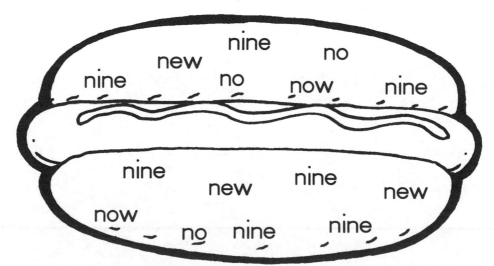

nine
new
nine   no
no   now   nine
nine   nine
new   new
now
no   nine   nine

See. Say. Rainbow trace.

Cut and Paste.

o n   o n

Trace and print.

no   no   no   no

_____ _____ _____ _____

WORD SEARCH
Circle the words "no."

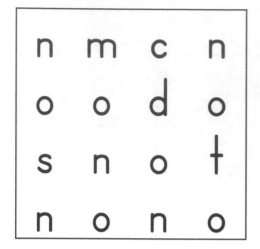

PYRAMID WORDS
Build a pyramid for the word "no."

-4-

1. _____ n̈

2. _____ _____

(The first letter goes on the top line. The first and second letters go on the second line and so on.)

MISSING LETTERS: Fill in the missing letters for the word "no."

-5-

COLORING WORDS: Color all of the sections that have the word "no."

-6-

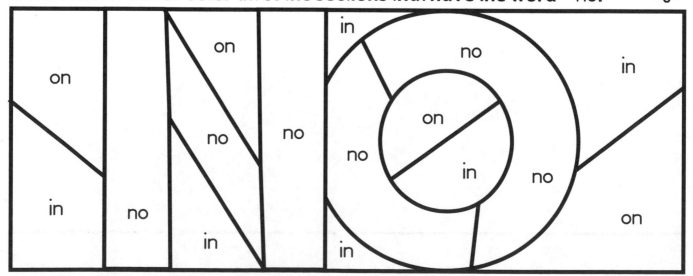

See. Say. Rainbow trace.

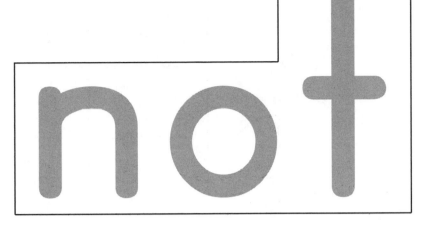

Cut and Paste.

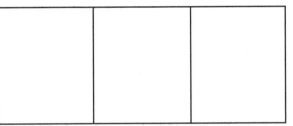

o	n	t

t	o	n

Trace and print.

not   not   not   not

_____   _____   _____   _____

BLEND THE WORD
Draw a line to make the word "not."

TIC-TAC-TOE
Circle the letters that spell "not."

n	u	m
o	f	s
t	e	r

LETTER CONNECT
Connect the letters that spell "not."

PYRAMID WORDS
Build a pyramid for the word "not."

1. _____

2. _____ _____

3. _____ _____ _____

(The first letter goes on the top line. The first and second letters go on the second line and so on.)

FINISH THE SENTENCE
Use the word "not" to fill in the blanks. Read each sentence.

1. The dog did _____ come home.

2. I did _____ see him.

3. You should _____ be late.

Cut and Paste. ✂ **-2-**

o   w   n   n   w   o

Trace and print. ✏ **-3-**

now   now   now   now

_____   _____   _____   _____

TIC-TAC-TOE
Circle the letters that spell "now."

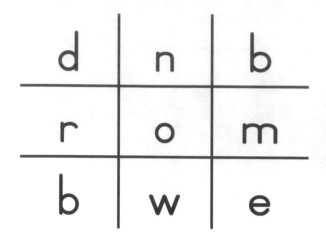

d	n	b
r	o	m
b	w	e

LETTER MAZE
Circle the letters that spell "now."

MISSING LETTERS: Fill in the missing letters for the word " now."

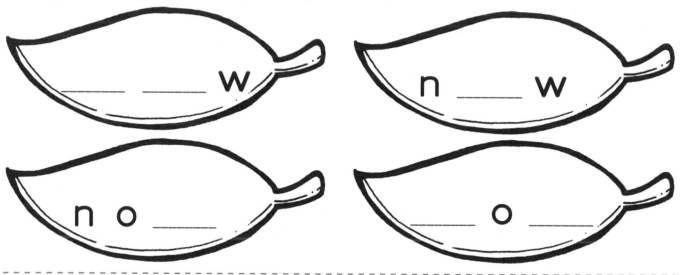

___ ___ w

n ___ w

n o ___

___ o ___

COLORING WORDS: Color all of the leaves that have the word " now."

See. Say. Rainbow trace.

Cut and Paste.

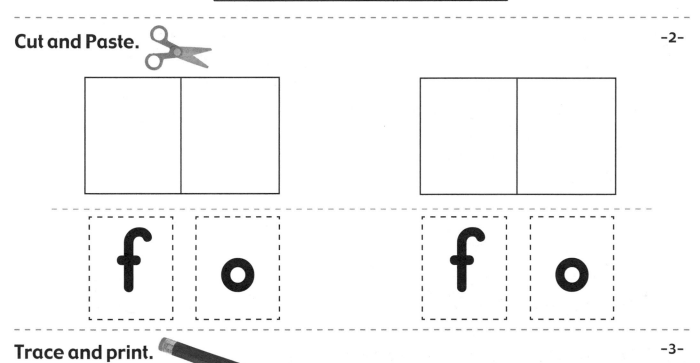

Trace and print.

of   of   of   of

_____   _____   _____   _____

MISSING LETTERS
Fill in the missing letters for the word " of."

_____ f

o _____

o _____

_____ f

of	at	on
as	of	on
on	as	of

WORD MAZE
Circle the words that spell " of."

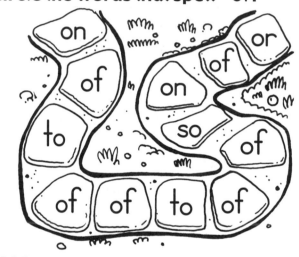

to on of of it off
is of of so
so of of
or to of so
on is of is on

See. Say. Rainbow trace.

Cut and Paste.

n   o   n   o

Trace and print.

on   on   on   on

_____ _____ _____ _____

PYRAMID WORDS
Build a pyramid for the word "on."

1. _____

2. _____ _____

(The first letter goes on the top line. The first and second letters go on the second line and so on.)

WORD TIC-TAC-TOE
Circle the words "on."

of	am	an
an	at	of
on	on	on

LETTER CONNECT
Connect the letters that spell "on."

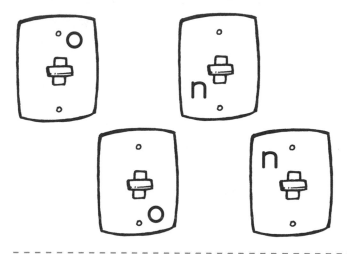

DOT-TO-DOT
Connect the letters that spell "on."

FINISH THE SENTENCE
Use the word "on" to fill in the blanks. Read each sentence.

1. The book is _____ the table.

2. She put the hat _____ .

3. Please turn the light _____ .

one

Cut and Paste. ✂ -2-

| | | | | | | |

| e | o | n | | n | o | e |

Trace and print. ✏ -3-

one   one   one   one

_____ _____ _____ _____

TIC-TAC-TOE
Circle the letters that spell " one."

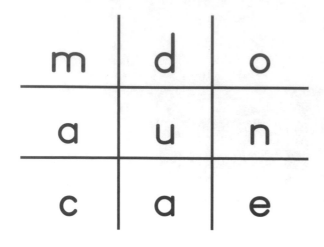

m	d	o
a	u	n
c	a	e

LETTER MAZE
Circle the letters that spell " one."

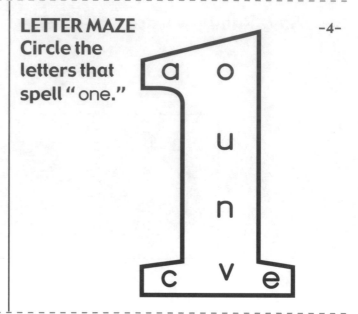

MISSING LETTERS: Fill in the missing letters for the word " one."

o n ____

o ____ n ____

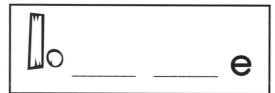

o ____ ____ e

o ____ e

SPELL IT! Circle all of the words that spell " one."

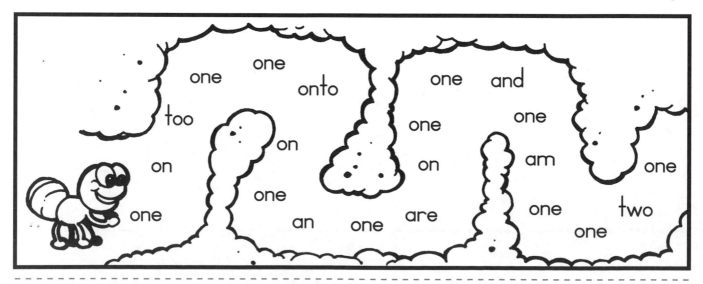

one one onto one and too one one on on am one one an one are one two one

---

or

r   o   r   o

or   or   or   or

_____   _____   _____   _____

WORD SEARCH
Circle the words "or."

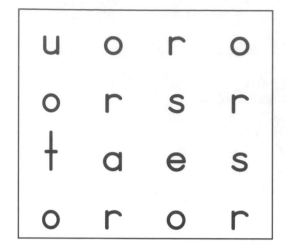

PYRAMID WORDS −4−
Build a pyramid for the word "or."

1. ___ ⚬ ___

2. _____ _____

(The first letter goes on the top line. The first and second letters go on the second line and so on.)

MISSING LETTERS: Fill in the missing letters for the word "or." −5−

COLORING WORDS: Color all of the pineapples that have the word "or." −6−

Cut and Paste. ✂ -2-

n   r   a   o   e g

Trace and print. ✏ -3-

orange   orange   orange

_____   _____   _____

BLEND THE WORD
Draw a line to make the word "orange."

oran
ora
or
o

ge
ange
range
nge

WORD TIC-TAC-TOE
Circle the words "orange."

orange	only	people
orange	one	only
orange	one	people

LETTER MAZE
Connect the letters that spell "orange."

e   o   a

r   n   g

DOT-TO-DOT
Connect the letters that spell "orange."

o   e

r   g

a   n

FINISH THE SENTENCE
Use the word "orange" to fill in the blanks. Read each sentence.

1. I like the color _____ .

2. I want to eat an _____ .

3. I have an _____ book.

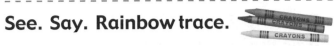

our

Cut and Paste. ✂ -2-

r o u u r o

Trace and print. ✏ -3-

our our our our

_____ _____ _____ _____

TIC-TAC-TOE
Circle the letters that spell "our."

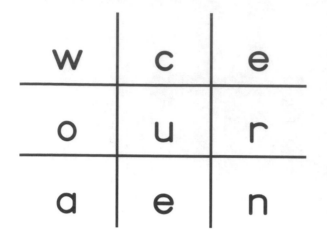

w	c	e
o	u	r
a	e	n

LETTER MAZE
Circle the letters that spell "our."

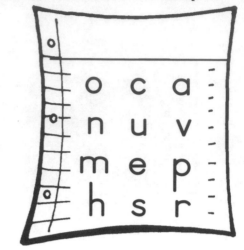

o c a
n u v
m e p
h s r

MISSING LETTERS: Fill in the missing letters for the word "our."

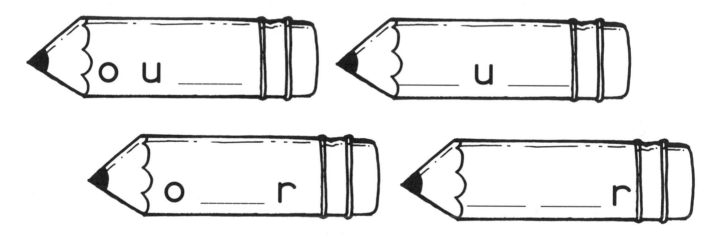

o u ___

u ___

o ___ r

___ r

COLORING WORDS: Color all of the sections that have the word "our."

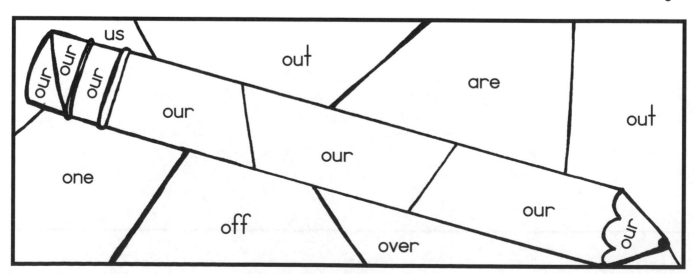

us
our
our
our
out
are
our
out
our
one
off
over
our
our

See. Say. Rainbow trace.

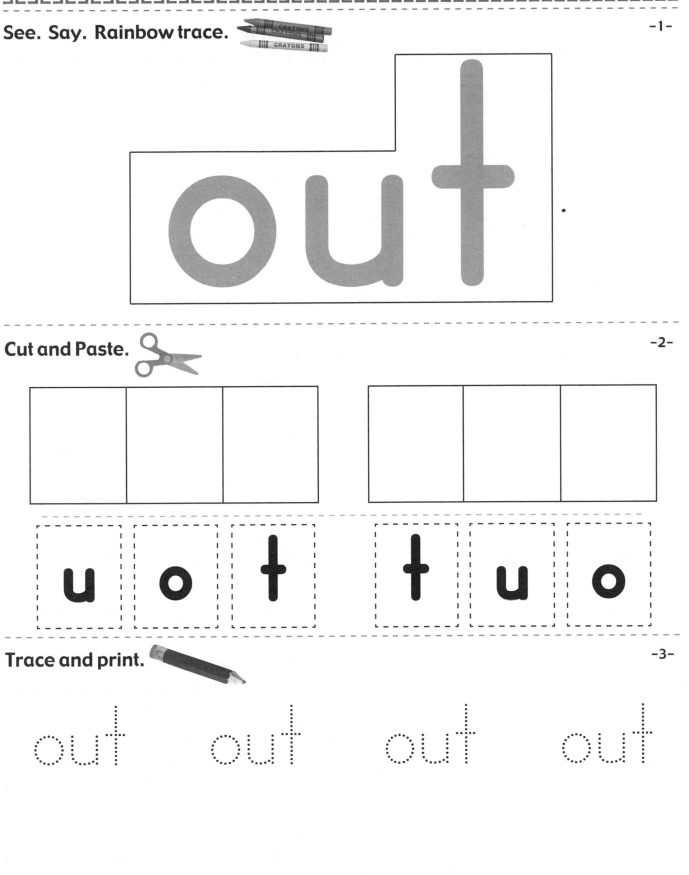

Cut and Paste.

u   o   t   t   u   o

Trace and print.

out   out   out   out

WORD SEARCH
Circle the words "out."

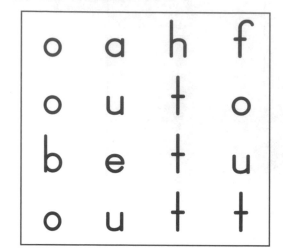

```
o  a  h     f
o  u  t     o
b  e  t     u
o  u  t     t
```

PYRAMID WORDS
-4-
Build a pyramid for the word "out."

1. __○____

2. _____ _____

3. _____ _____ _____

(The first letter goes on the top line. The first and second letters go on the second line and so on.)

SCRAMBLED WORDS: Unscramble the letters to spell the word "out."   -5-

 tuo

 uto

 otu

 tou

_____   _____   _____   _____

COLORING WORDS: Color all of the seals that have the word "out."   -6-

Cut and Paste. ✂ -2-

v	r	o	e

Trace and print. ✏ -3-

over   over   over

_____   _____   _____

BLEND THE WORD
Draw a line to make the word "over."

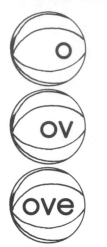

WORD TIC-TAC-TOE
Circle the words "over."

only	above	one
of	one	after
over	over	over

LETTER CONNECT
Connect the letters that spell "over."

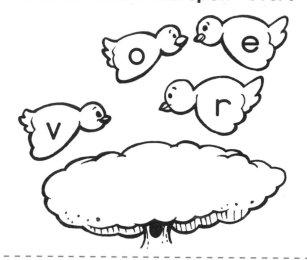

LETTER MAZE

Circle the letters that spell "over."
How many "over" words did you find?

_____

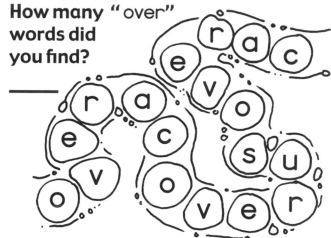

FINISH THE SENTENCE

Use the word "over" to fill in the blanks. Read each sentence.

1. The bird is _____ the tree.

2. The show is _____ .

3. Let's go _____ to his house.

See. Say. Rainbow trace.

people

Cut and Paste. ✂

e p l o e p

Trace and print. ✏

people   people   people

_____   _____   _____

WORD TIC-TAC-TOE
Circle the words "people."

please	please	people
purple	pink	people
purple	pink	people

PYRAMID WORDS
-4-
Build a pyramid for the word "people."

1. P
2. ___ ___
3. ___ ___ ___
4. ___ ___ ___ ___
5. ___ ___ ___ ___ ___
6. ___ ___ ___ ___ ___ ___

(The first letter goes on the top line. The first and second letters go on the second line and so on.)

MISSING LETTERS:
Fill in the missing letters for the word "people."
-5-

___ e ___ p ___ e

p ___ ___ ___ l e

___ e ___ ___ l e

p ___ o ___ l ___

COLORING WORDS: Color all of the shirts that have the word "people." -6-

See. Say. Rainbow trace.

play

l a y p

play play play play

_____ _____ _____ _____

WORD SEARCH
Circle the words "play."

p	l	a	y	p
d	l	e	o	l
c	s	a	r	a
p	l	a	y	y
d	o	w	v	e

PYRAMID WORDS
-4-
Build a pyramid for the word "play."

1. ___p___

2. _____ _____

3. _____ _____ _____

4. _____ _____ _____ _____

(The first letter goes on the top line. The first and second letters go on the second line and so on.)

SCRAMBLED WORDS: Unscramble the letters to spell the word "play." -5-

payl

aypl

lapy

lyap

_____ _____ _____

SPELL IT! Circle all of the words that spell "play." -6-

**See. Say.
Rainbow trace.**

please

Cut and Paste.

e p l s e a

Trace and print.

please   please   please

BLEND THE WORD
Draw a line to make the word "please."

pl	se
ple	ease
pleas	e
plea	ase

WORD TIC-TAC-TOE
Circle the words "please."

pink	please	people
purple	please	pink
people	please	purple

LETTER CONNECT
Connect the letters that spell "please."

e l
p a
s e

DOT-TO-DOT
Connect the letters that spell "please."

e a s
l
p
e

FINISH THE SENTENCE
Use the word "please" to fill in the blanks. Read each sentence.

1. _____ sit over there.

2. _____ come to my house.

3. She said, "_____ ."

See. Say. Rainbow trace.

pretty

Cut and Paste.

e p t y t r

Trace and print.

pretty   pretty   pretty

_____   _____   _____

WORD TIC-TAC-TOE
Circle the words "pretty."

please	pink	blue
pretty	pretty	pretty
blue	pink	please

-4-

LETTER MAZE
Circle the letters that spell "pretty."

MISSING LETTERS: Fill in the missing letters for the word "pretty." -5-

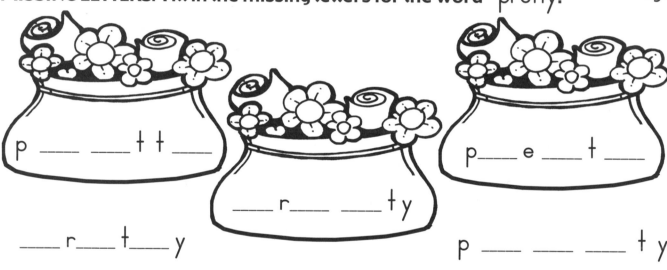

p ___ ___ t t ___

___ r ___ t ___ y

___ r ___ ___ t y

p ___ e ___ t ___

p ___ ___ ___ t y

COLORING WORDS: Color all of the gloves that have the word "pretty." -6-

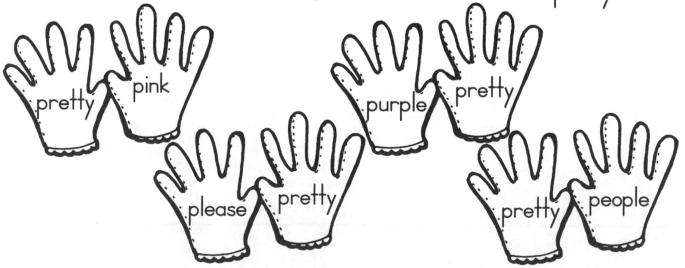

pretty pink please pretty purple pretty pretty people

See. Say. Rainbow trace. -1-

purple

Cut and Paste. ✂ -2-

r p l u e p

Trace and print. -3-

purple   purple   purple

_____ _____

KE-804038 © Key Education -231- *The Best Sight Word Book Ever!*

WORD SEARCH
Circle the words "purple."

p	u	r	p	l	e
d	u	s	u	e	t
g	o	r	r	t	f
p	u	r	p	l	e
o	r	s	l	l	n
v	z	w	e	r	e

PYRAMID WORDS
-4-

Build a pyramid for the word "purple."

1. p̣ _
2. ___ ___
3. ___ ___ ___
4. ___ ___ ___ ___
5. ___ ___ ___ ___ ___
6. ___ ___ ___ ___ ___ ___

(The first letter goes on the top line. The first and second letters go on the second line and so on.)

SCRAMBLED WORDS: Unscramble the letters to spell the word "purple." -5-

_____   _____   _____   _____

COLORING WORDS: Color all of the grapes that have the word "purple." -6-

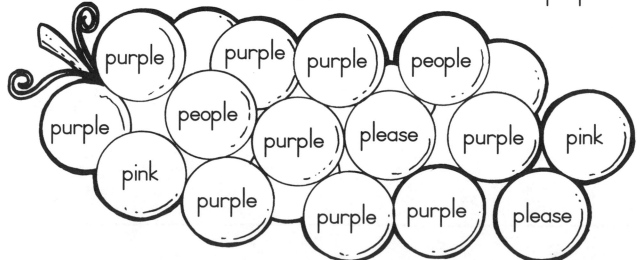

put

Cut and Paste. -2-

| t | u | p |

| p | t | u |

Trace and print. -3-

put   put   put   put

___ ___ ___ ___

BLEND THE WORD
Draw a line to make the word "put."

TIC-TAC-TOE
−4−

Circle the letters that spell "put."

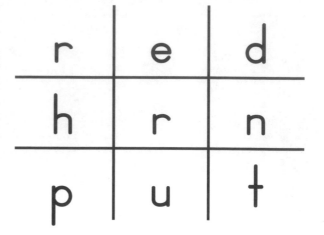

LETTER CONNECT
Connect the letters that spell "put."

LETTER MAZE
−5−

Circle the letters that spell "put."

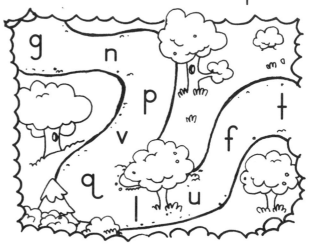

FINISH THE SENTENCE
−6−

Use the word "put" to fill in the blanks. Read each sentence.

1. Mom _____ the dog outside.

2. _____ the book on the table.

3. Please, _____ the cat down.

See. Say. Rainbow trace.  -1-

Cut and Paste. ✂ -2-

| | | | | | | |

a r n n r a

Trace and print. ✏ -3-

ran   ran   ran   ran

_____ _____ _____ _____

TIC–TAC–TOE
Circle the letters that spell "ran."

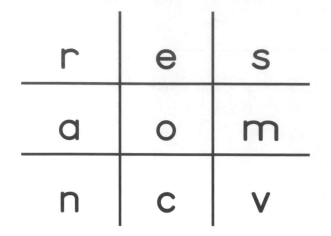

r	e	s
a	o	m
n	c	v

LETTER MAZE
Circle the letters that spell "ran."

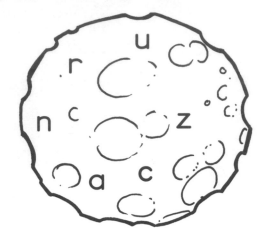

MISSING LETTERS: Fill in the missing letters for the word "ran."

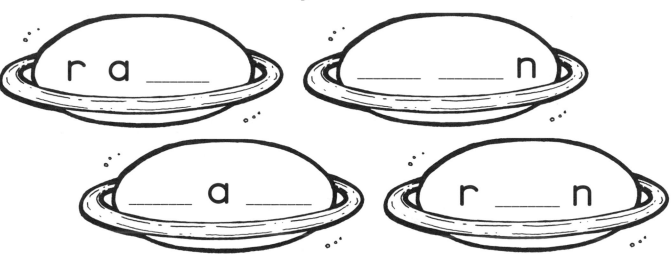

r a ____

____ ____ n

____ a ____

r ____ n

SPELL IT! Circle all of the words that spell "ran."

See. Say. Rainbow trace. -1-

red

Cut and Paste. -2-

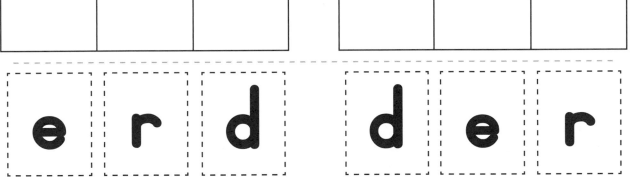

| e | r | d | d | e | r |

Trace and print. -3-

red   red   red   red

_____   _____   _____   _____

WORD SEARCH
Circle the words "red."

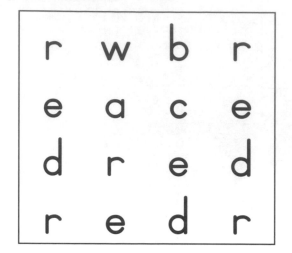

r w b r
e a c e
d r e d
r e d r

PYRAMID WORDS
Build a pyramid for the word "red."   -4-

1. ___ r

2. _____ _____

3. _____ _____ _____

(The first letter goes on the top line. The first and second letters go on the second line and so on.)

SCRAMBLED WORDS: Unscramble the letters to spell the word "red."   -5-

rde   dre   erd   der

_____   _____   _____   _____

COLORING WORDS: Color all of the sections that have the word "red."   -6-

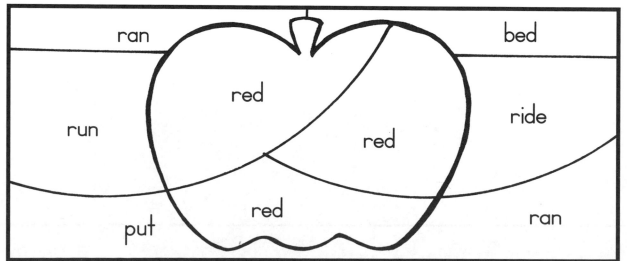

ran   bed
red
run   ride
red
put   red   ran

See. Say. Rainbow trace.

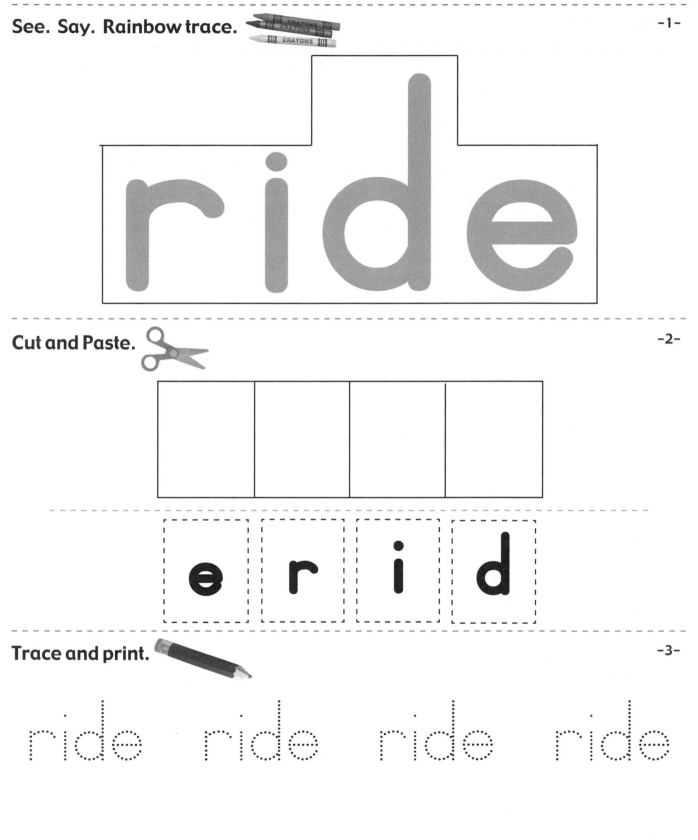

ride

Cut and Paste.

e   r   i   d

Trace and print.

ride   ride   ride   ride

_____   _____   _____   _____

BLEND THE WORD
Draw a line to make the word "ride."

WORD TIC-TAC-TOE
Circle the words "ride."

ride	red	run
run	ride	ran
red	run	ride

LETTER CONNECT
Connect the letters that spell "ride."

DOT-TO-DOT
Connect the letters that spell "ride."

FINISH THE SENTENCE
Use the word "ride" to fill in the blanks. Read each sentence.

1. I want to _____ a horse.

2. We know how to _____ a bike.

3. We _____ the bus to school.

See. Say. Rainbow trace.

run

Cut and Paste. ✂

u	r	n

n	r	u

Trace and print. ✏

run　　run　　run　　run

_____ _____ _____ _____

TIC-TAC-TOE
Circle the letters that spell "run."

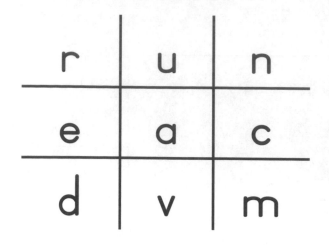

r	u	n
e	a	c
d	v	m

PYRAMID WORDS
Build a pyramid for the word "run."

1. _____

2. _____ _____

3. _____ _____ _____

(The first letter goes on the top line. The first and second letters go on the second line and so on.)

MISSING LETTERS: Fill in the missing letters for the word "run."

r u ___   ___ u ___

r ___ n   ___ ___ n

SPELL IT! Circle all of the words that spell "run."

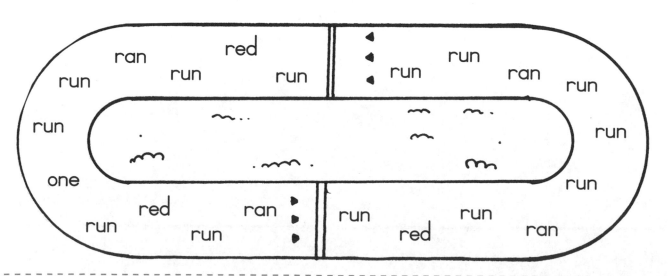

ran red run
run run run ran run
run
one run run
red ran run run ran
run run red run

See. Say. Rainbow trace.

said

Cut and Paste.

d s a i

Trace and print.

said   said   said   said

_____   _____   _____   _____

WORD SEARCH
Circle the words " said."

r	s	a	i	d
s	s	z	j	n
a	s	a	i	d
i	w	v	i	x
d	r	s	b	d

PYRAMID WORDS
-4-
Build a pyramid for the word " said."

1. ___s___

2. _____ _____

3. _____ _____ _____

4. _____ _____ _____ _____

(The first letter goes on the top line. The first and second letters go on the second line and so on.)

SCRAMBLED WORDS: Unscramble the letters to spell the word " said."   -5-

dsai   sdia   dias   adsi

_____   _____   _____   _____

COLORING WORDS: Color all of the socks that have the word " said."   -6-

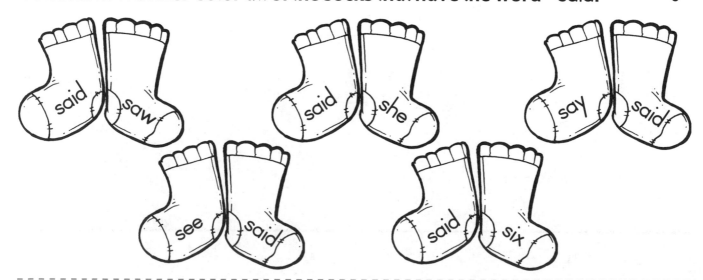

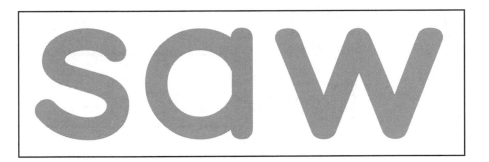

Cut and Paste. ✂ -2-

a s w w s a

Trace and print. -3-

saw   saw   saw   saw

_____ _____ _____ _____ _____

BLEND THE WORD
Draw a line to make the word " saw."

TIC-TAC-TOE
-4-

Circle the letters that spell " saw."

r	z	v
s	a	w
m	v	n

LETTER CONNECT
Connect the letters that spell " saw."

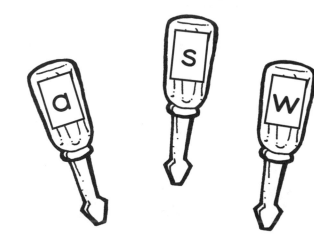

DOT-TO-DOT
-5-

Connect the letters that spell " saw."

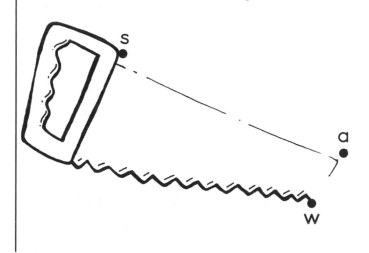

FINISH THE SENTENCE
-6-

Use the word " saw" to fill in the blanks. Read each sentence.

1. I _____ the car go by.

2. I _____ the dog play.

3. We _____ the new teacher.

See. Say. Rainbow trace.

Cut and Paste.

a s y   y s a

Trace and print.

say   say   say   say

_____ _____ _____ _____

TIC-TAC-TOE
Circle the letters that spell "say."

n	c	b
s	a	y
z	p	j

WORD MAZE
Circle the word "say."

MISSING LETTERS Fill in the missing letters for the word "say."

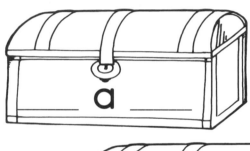

a _____

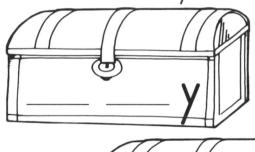

_____ y

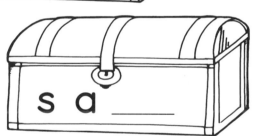

s a _____

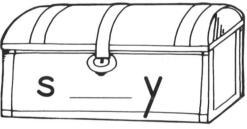

s _____ y

COLORING WORDS: Color all of the seahorses that have the word "say."

See. Say. Rainbow trace.

school

Cut and Paste.

o   s   l   h   c   o

Trace and print.

school   school   school

_____   _____   _____

WORD SEARCH
Circle the words "school."

s	z	b	d	t	s
c	c	v	c	n	c
h	q	h	h	z	h
o	u	m	o	w	o
o	a	f	o	o	o
l	k	d	l	f	l

PYRAMID WORDS
Build a pyramid for the word "school." -4-

1. __s__
2. ____ ____
3. ____ ____ ____
4. ____ ____ ____ ____
5. ____ ____ ____ ____ ____
6. ____ ____ ____ ____ ____ ____

(The first letter goes on the top line. The first and second letters go on the second line and so on.)

SCRAMBLED WORDS: Unscramble the letters to spell the word "school." -5-

solhco   oolchs   hosclo   sholco

_____ _____ _____ _____

COLORING WORDS: Color all of the schoolhouses that have the word "school." -6-

seven   school   school

school   school   some

Cut and Paste. ✂ –2–

e   s   e   e   e   s

Trace and print. –3–

see   see   see   see

BLEND THE WORD
Draw a line to make the word "see."

s

e

se

ee

TIC-TAC-TOE
Circle the letters that spell "see."

s	e	e
z	a	m
o	r	a

PYRAMID WORDS
Build a pyramid for the word "see."

1. ___s___

2. _____ _____

3. _____ _____ _____

(The first letter goes on the top line. The first and second letters go on the second line and so on.)

WORD MAZE
Circle all of the words "see."

s

e

s   e

s   e   e   e   e

s   e

s

e   e
s   s
e   s
s   e

FINISH THE SENTENCE
Use the word "see" to fill in the blanks. Read each sentence.

1. We can _____ the dog.

2. Did you _____ the cat?

3. Come over and _____ my dog.

See. Say. Rainbow trace.

seven

Cut and Paste.

e v s e n

Trace and print.

seven   seven   seven

_____   _____   _____

WORD TIC–TAC–TOE
Circle the words " seven."

seven	she	some
seven	some	some
seven	sent	she

LETTER MAZE
Circle the letters that spell "seven."

MISSING LETTERS: Fill in the missing letters for the word " seven."

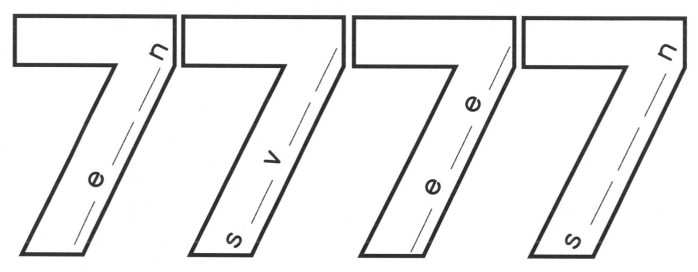

COLORING WORDS: Color all of the balls that have the word " seven."

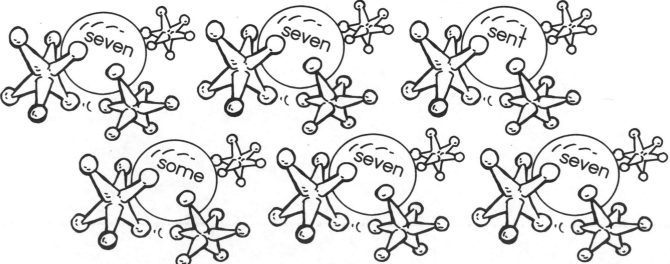

See. Say. Rainbow trace.

she

Cut and Paste.

s   e   h   h   e   s

Trace and print.

she   she   she   she

WORD SEARCH
Circle the words "she."

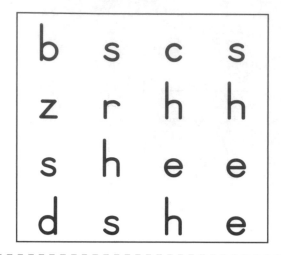

b	s	c	s
z	r	h	h
s	h	e	e
d	s	h	e

PYRAMID WORDS
Build a pyramid for the word "she." -4-

1. ___s___

2. _____ _____

3. _____ _____ _____

(The first letter goes on the top line. The first and second letters go on the second line and so on.)

SCRAMBLED WORDS: Unscramble the letters to spell the word "she." -5-

hse   hes   esh   ehs

_____   _____   _____   _____

SPELL IT! Circle all of the words that spell "she." -6-

See. Say. Rainbow trace.

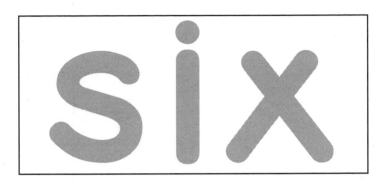

Cut and Paste.

i s x   x i s

Trace and print.

six   six   six   six

_____ _____ _____ _____

PYRAMID WORDS
Build a pyramid for the word "six."

1. ___s___

2. _____ _____

3. _____ _____ _____

(The first letter goes on the top line. The first and second letters go on the second line and so on.)

TIC-TAC-TOE   -4-
Circle the letters that spell "six."

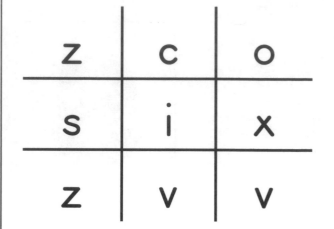

LETTER CONNECT
Connect the letters that spell "six."

DOT-TO-DOT   -5-
Connect the letters that spell "six."

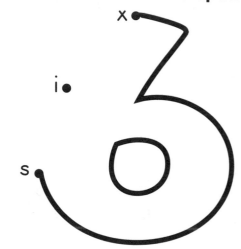

FINISH THE SENTENCE   -6-
Use the word "six" to fill in the blanks. Read each sentence.

1. I have read _____ books.

2. My sister is _____ years old.

3. I have _____ pets.

See. Say. Rainbow trace.

SO

Cut and Paste. ✂

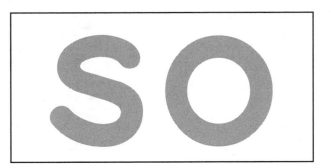

o   s   o   s

Trace and print. ✏

SO   SO   SO   SO

_____ _____ _____ _____

WORD TIC-TAC-TOE
Circle the words " so."

do	go	to
go	to	do
so	so	so

WORD MAZE
Circle the words " so."

MISSING LETTERS: Fill in the missing letters for the word " so." -5-

s ___   ___ o   s ___   ___ o

WORD MAZE: Circle all of the words that spell " so." -6-

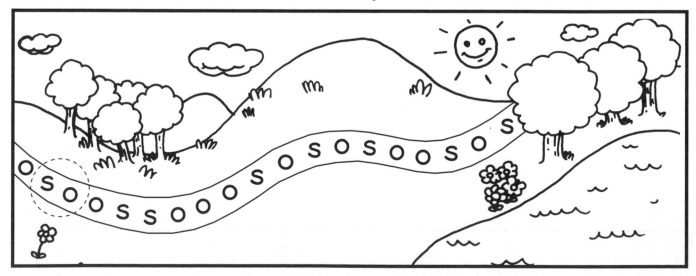

Cut and Paste. -2-

m s o e

Trace and print. -3-

some   some   some

_____   _____   _____

WORD SEARCH
Circle the words "some."

s	s	c	z	s
s	o	m	e	o
o	m	m	x	m
m	e	d	e	e
e	z	n	r	c

PYRAMID WORDS

Build a pyramid for the word "some."

1. ___s___

2. _____ _____

3. _____ _____ _____

4. _____ _____ _____ _____

(The first letter goes on the top line. The first and second letters go on the second line and so on.)

SCRAMBLED WORDS: Unscramble the letters to spell the word "some." –5–

esmo

omes

seom

osem

SPELL IT! Circle all of the words that spell "some." –6–

some
some
soon
sent
some
so
some
she
some
soon

See. Say. Rainbow trace.

Cut and Paste. ✂

o s o n

Trace and print. ✏

soon soon soon

BLEND THE WORD
Draw a line to make the word " soon."

soo

s

so

oon

on

n

WORD TIC-TAC-TOE
Circle the words " soon."

some	soon	she
seven	soon	sit
she	soon	some

PYRAMID WORDS
Build a pyramid for the word " soon."

1. ___s___

2. _____ _____

3. _____ _____ _____

4. _____ _____ _____ _____

(The first letter goes on the top line. The first and second letters go on the second line and so on.)

DOT-TO-DOT
Connect the letters that spell " soon."

FINISH THE SENTENCE
Use the word " soon" to fill in the blanks. Read each sentence.

1. I will be there _____ .

2. _____ it will be time for lunch.

3. I will call you _____ .

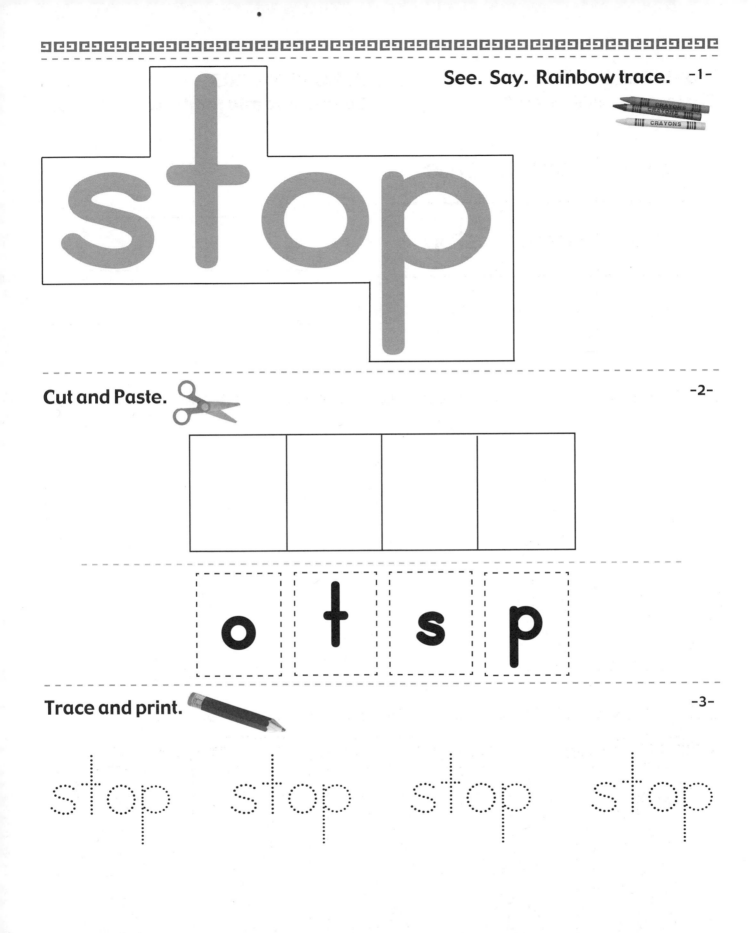

See. Say. Rainbow trace. -1-

stop

Cut and Paste. -2-

o t s p

Trace and print. -3-

stop stop stop stop

WORD TIC-TAC-TOE
Circle the words "stop."

seven	some	stop
soon	some	stop
six	soon	stop

PYRAMID WORDS
−4−

Build a pyramid for the word "stop."

1. ___ s ___

2. ___ ___ ___

3. ___ ___ ___ ___

4. ___ ___ ___ ___ ___

(The first letter goes on the top line. The first and second letters go on the second line and so on.)

MISSING LETTERS: Fill in the missing letters for the word "stop."
−5−

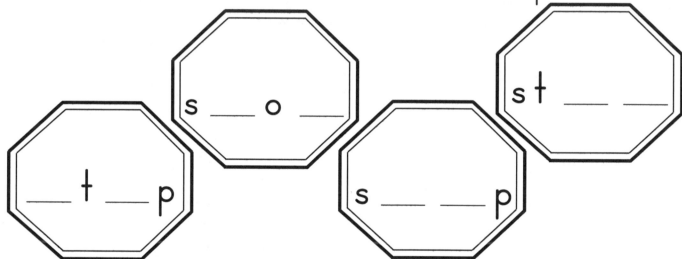

COLORING WORDS: Color all of the circles that have the word "stop."
−6−

See. Say. Rainbow trace.

Cut and Paste.

k   t   e   a

Trace and print.

take   take   take   take

_____   _____   _____   _____

WORD SEARCH
Circle the words "take."

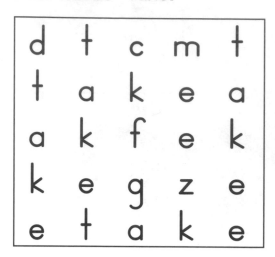

d	t	c	m	t
t	a	k	e	a
a	k	f	e	k
k	e	g	z	e
e	t	a	k	e

PYRAMID WORDS
-4-
Build a pyramid for the word "take."

1. _____

2. _____ _____

3. _____ _____ _____

4. _____ _____ _____ _____

(The first letter goes on the top line. The first and second letters go on the second line and so on.)

SCRAMBLED WORDS: Unscramble the letters to spell the word "take." -5-

ktae   keat   eatk   taek

_____   _____

COLORING WORDS: Color all of the foods that have the word "take." -6-

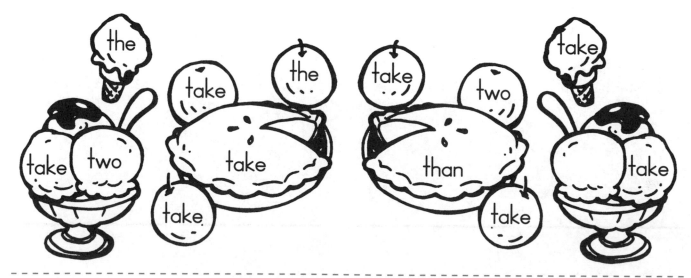

See. Say. Rainbow trace.

Cut and Paste.

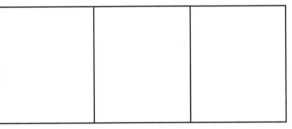 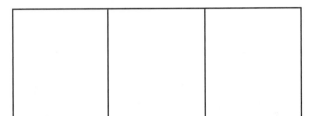

Trace and print.

_____ _____ _____ _____

PYRAMID WORDS
Build a pyramid for the word "ten."

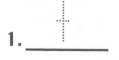

1. _____

2. _____ _____

3. _____ _____ _____

(The first letter goes on the top line. The first and second letters go on the second line and so on.)

TIC-TAC-TOE
-4-

Circle the letters that spell "ten."

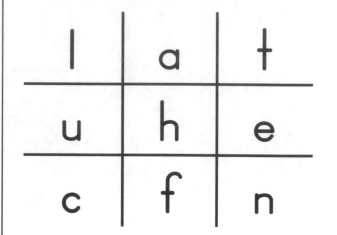

WORD MAZE
Circle the words that spell "ten."

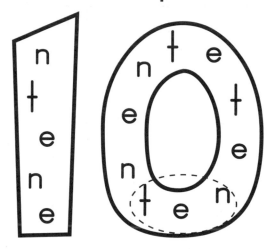

DOT-TO-DOT
-5-

Connect the letters that spell "ten."

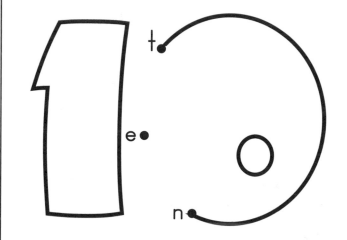

FINISH THE SENTENCE
-6-

Use the word "ten" to fill in the blanks. Read each sentence.

1. I have _____ toes.

2. My birthday is in _____ days.

3. I have _____ good friends.

See. Say. Rainbow trace.

Cut and Paste.

a t h n

Trace and print.

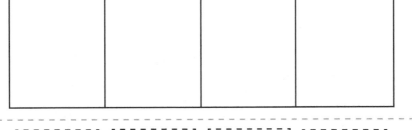

than than than than

_____ _____ _____ _____

WORD TIC-TAC-TOE
Circle the words "than."

then	the	then
than	than	than
that	that	those

BLEND THE WORD
Draw a line to make the word "than." -4-

MISSING LETTERS: Fill in the missing letters for the word "than." -5-

COLORING WORDS: Color all of the eels that have the word "than." -6-

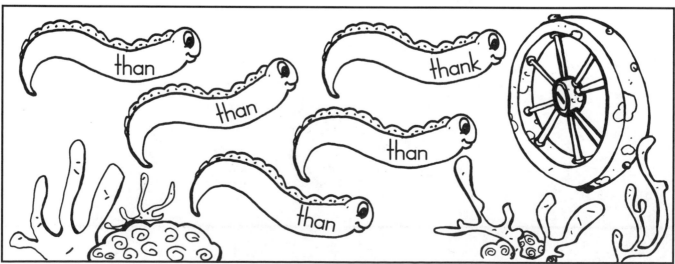

See. Say. Rainbow trace.

thank

Cut and Paste.

a h n k t

Trace and print.

thank thank thank

_____ _____ _____

WORD SEARCH
Circle the words "thank."

t	t	h	a	n	k
h	t	d	u	t	f
a	h	h	f	h	b
n	a	c	a	a	z
k	n	u	z	n	r
e	k	r	s	k	k

PYRAMID WORDS
-4-
Build a pyramid for the word "thank."

1. ___
2. ___ ___
3. ___ ___ ___
4. ___ ___ ___ ___
5. ___ ___ ___ ___ ___

(The first letter goes on the top line. The first and second letters go on the second line and so on.)

SCRAMBLED WORDS: Unscramble the letters to spell the word "thank." -5-

nakth _____

hntak _____

_____ tanhk

_____ ankht

COLORING WORDS: Color all of the sandwiches that have the word "thank." -6-

thank / than

thin / thank

the / thank

this / thank

thank / then

See. Say. Rainbow trace.  -1-

- -

Cut and Paste.   -2-

- -

Trace and print.  -3-

that   that   that   that

_____   _____   _____   _____

BLEND THE WORD
Draw a line to make the word "that."

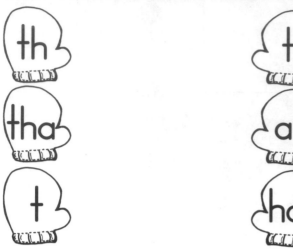

thank	thank	that
than	then	that
than	than	that

LETTER CONNECT
Connect the letters that spell "that."

DOT-TO-DOT
Connect the letters that spell "that."

-5-

FINISH THE SENTENCE
Use the word "that" to fill in the blanks. Read each sentence.

-6-

1. I did not see _____ .

2. I think _____ will be fun.

3. Where did _____ dog go?

See. Say. Rainbow trace.

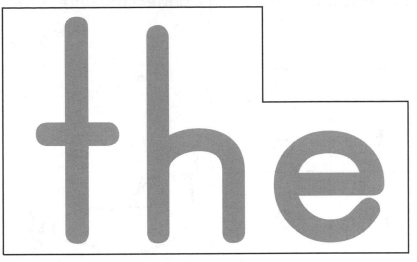

Cut and Paste.

Trace and print.

the   the   the   the

_____   _____   _____   _____

TIC-TAC-TOE
Circle the letters that spell "the."

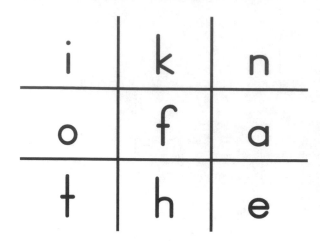

i	k	n
o	f	a
t	h	e

DOT-TO-DOT
Connect the letters that spell "the."

MISSING LETTERS: Fill in the missing letters for the word "the."

COLORING FUN! Color all of the boots that have the word "the."

 The Best Sight Word Book Ever!

See. Say. Rainbow trace.

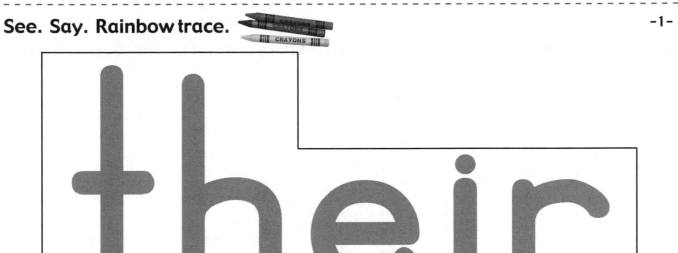

Cut and Paste.

Trace and print.

WORD SEARCH
Circle the words "their."

```
f  g  c  s  t  a
d  w  h  t  h  o
r  o  m  h  e  v
l  t  h  e  i  r
t  h  e  i  r  p
f  t  h  e  i  r
```

PYRAMID WORDS
Build a pyramid for the word "their."

-4-

1. ____

2. ____ ____

3. ____ ____ ____

4. ____ ____ ____ ____

5. ____ ____ ____ ____ ____

(The first letter goes on the top line. The first and second letters go on the second line and so on.)

SCRAMBLED WORDS: Unscramble the letters to spell the word "their."   -5-

rieth   teirh   tehri   reith

COLORING WORDS: Color all of the ponies that have the word "their."   -6-

the   their   their

their   their   then

See. Say. Rainbow trace.

Cut and Paste.

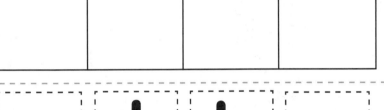

Trace and print.

them them them them

_____ _____ _____ _____

BLEND THE WORD
Draw a line to make the word "them."

WORD TIC-TAC-TOE
Circle the words "them."

them	then	than
them	that	the
them	the	then

LETTER CONNECT
Connect the letters that spell "them."

DOT-TO-DOT
Connect the letters that spell "them."

FINISH THE SENTENCE
Use the word "them" to fill in the blanks. Read each sentence.

1. I did not see _____ .

2. Look at all of _____ .

3. I like _____ a lot.

See. Say. Rainbow trace.

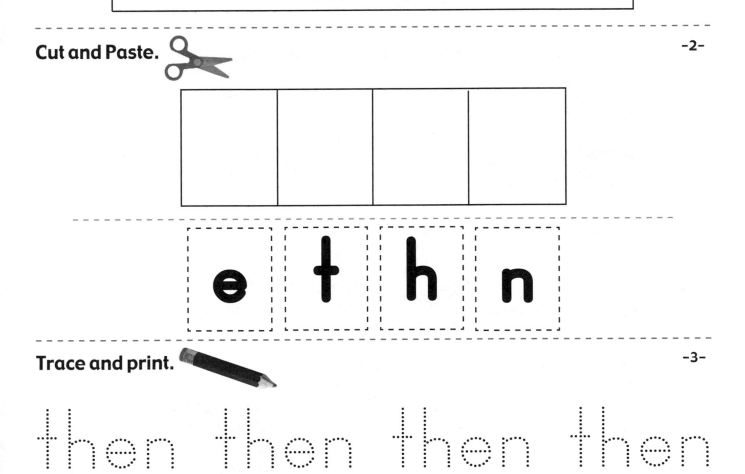

Cut and Paste.

e t h n

Trace and print.

then then then then

_____ _____ _____ _____

WORD TIC-TAC-TOE
Circle the words "then."

there	that	than
then	then	then
three	than	that

PYRAMID WORDS
Build a pyramid for the word "then." -4-

1. _____

2. _____ _____

3. _____ _____ _____

4. _____ _____ _____ _____

(The first letter goes on the top line. The first and second letters go on the second line and so on.)

MISSING LETTERS: Fill in the missing letters for the word "then." -5-

___ h ___ n

t h ___ ___

t ___ ___ n

t ___ ___ e

SPELL IT! Circle all of the words that spell "then." -6-

three

then

than

then

then

then

their

they

there

the

then

then

then

See. Say. Rainbow trace.

Cut and Paste.

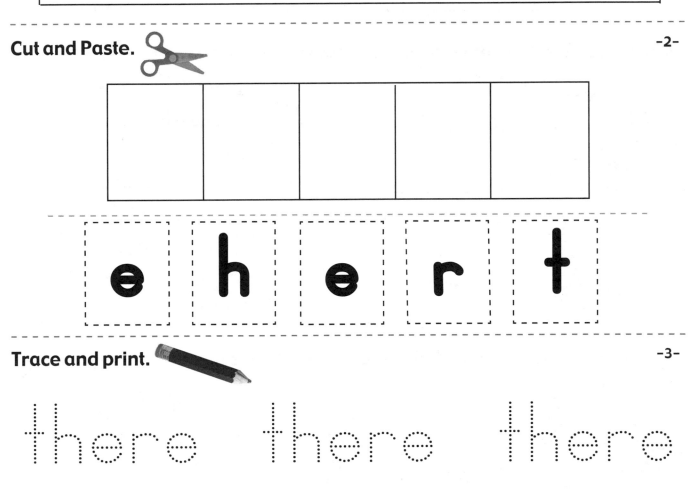

Trace and print.

there   there   there

WORD SEARCH
Circle the words " there."

t	h	e	r	e	r	e	t
h	f	z	c	o	h
e	t	h	e	r	e
r	n	r	w	m	r
e	z	p	l	u	e
t	h	e	r	e	d

PYRAMID WORDS
Build a pyramid for the word " there."   -4-

1. ___

2. ___ ___

3. ___ ___ ___

4. ___ ___ ___ ___

5. ___ ___ ___ ___ ___

(The first letter goes on the top line. The first and second letters go on the second line and so on.)

SCRAMBLED WORDS: Unscramble the letters to spell the word " there."   -5-

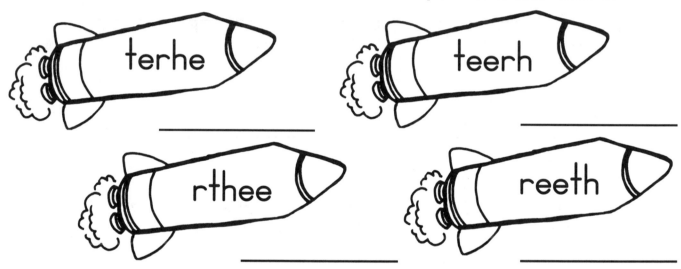

terhe

_____

teerh

_____

rthee

_____

reeth

_____

COLORING WORDS: Color all of the rockets that have the word " there."   -6-

there

three

there

there

their

then

there

See. Say. Rainbow trace. -1-

these

Cut and Paste. -2-

h s e e t

Trace and print. -3-

these   these   these

BLEND THE WORD
Draw a line to make the word "these."

 the

 th

t

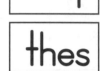 thes

 e

 hese

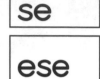 se

 ese

WORD TIC-TAC-TOE
Circle the words "these."

than	them	these
them	there	these
their	those	these

LETTER CONNECT
Connect the letters that spell "these."

DOT-TO-DOT
Connect the letters that spell "these."

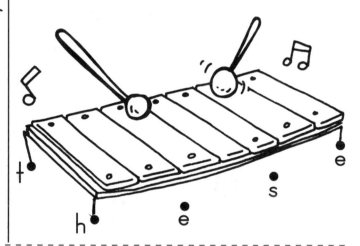

FINISH THE SENTENCE
Use the word "these" to fill in the blanks. Read each sentence.

1. Look at all _____ flowers.

2. Where did _____ books come from?

3. I like _____ pictures.

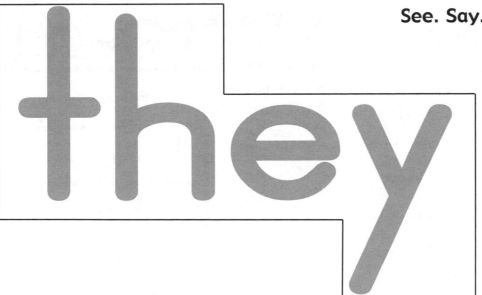

Cut and Paste. -2-

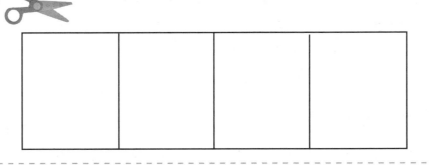

e t h y

Trace and print. -3-

they they they they

WORD TIC-TAC-TOE
Circle the words "they."

then	their	they
then	that	they
their	there	they

LETTER MAZE
Circle the letters in each line that spell "they."

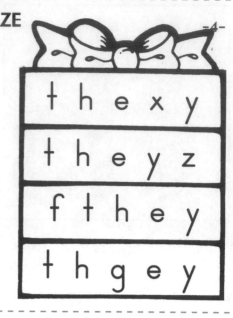

t	h	e	x	y
t	h	e	y	z
f	t	h	e	y
t	h	g	e	y

MISSING LETTERS: Fill in the missing letters for the word "they."

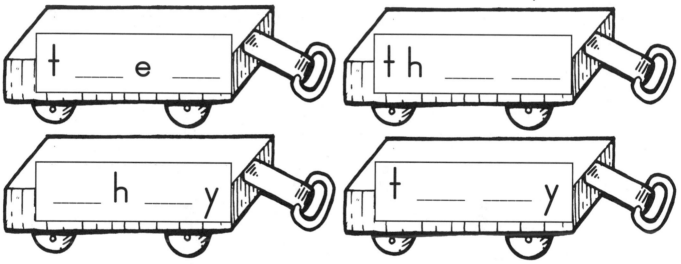

t __ e __

t h __ __

__ h __ y

t __ __ y

SPELL IT! Circle all of the words that spell "they."

See. Say. Rainbow trace.  -1-

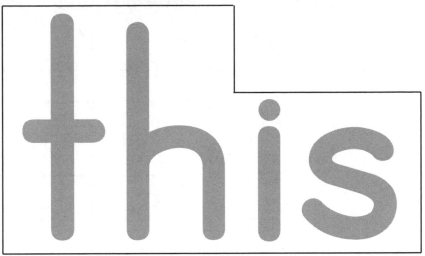

Cut and Paste. -2-

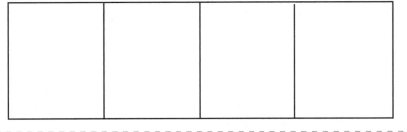

Trace and print. 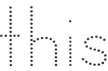 -3-

this this this this

_____ _____ _____ _____ _____

The Best Sight Word Book Ever!

BLEND THE WORD
Draw a line to make the word "this."

WORD TIC-TAC-TOE
Circle the words "this."

the	their	that
their	that	the
this	this	this

LETTER CONNECT
Connect the letters that spell "this."

DOT-TO-DOT
Connect the letters that spell "this."

FINISH THE SENTENCE
Use the word "this" to fill in the blanks. Read each sentence.

1. Where should I put _____ ?

2. I like _____ picture.

3. What do I do with _____ ?

See. Say. Rainbow trace.

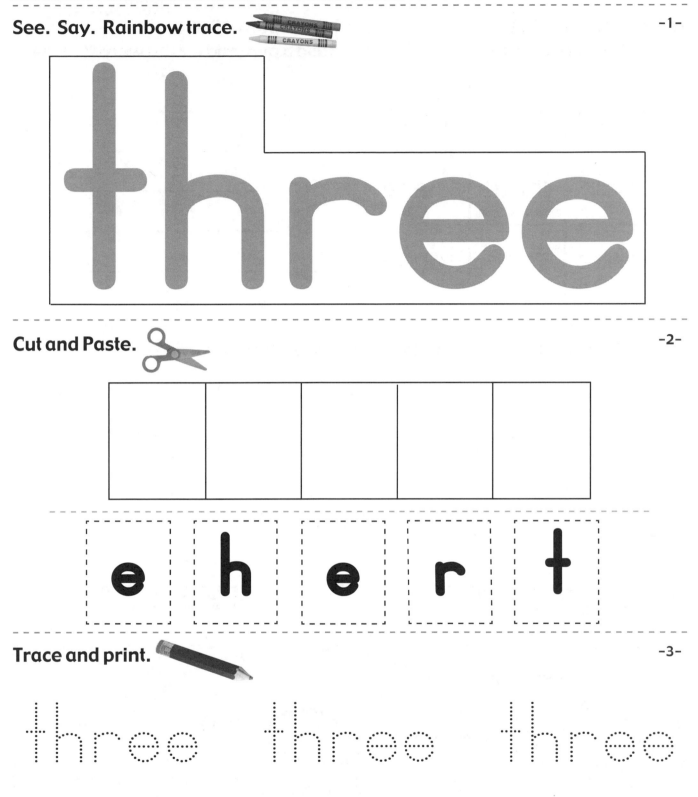

three

Cut and Paste.

e h e r t

Trace and print.

three three three

   The Best Sight Word Book Ever!

WORD TIC–TAC–TOE
Circle the words " three."

three	then	their
their	three	there
there	then	three

PYRAMID WORDS
Build a pyramid for the word " three."

1. ____
2. ____ ____
3. ____ ____ ____
4. ____ ____ ____ ____
5. ____ ____ ____ ____ ____

(The first letter goes on the top line. The first and second letters go on the second line and so on.)

MISSING LETTERS: Fill in the missing letters for the word " three."   -5-

___ h ___ ___ e
3 3 3 3 3 3 3 3 3

t ___ ___ ___ e
3 3 3 3 3 3 3 3 3

t ___ ___ e ___
3 3 3 3 3 3 3 3 3

t ___ r ___ ___
3 3 3 3 3 3 3 3 3

___ h ___ e ___
3 3 3 3 3 3 3 3 3

COLORING WORDS!
Color all of the sections that have the word " three."

-6-

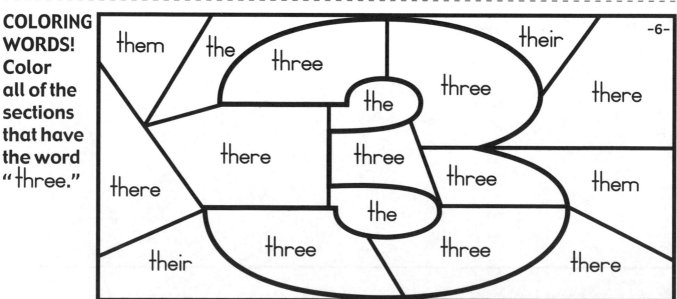

The Best Sight Word Book Ever!

Cut and Paste. -2-

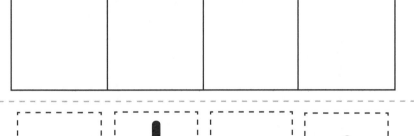

Trace and print. -3-

time time time time

WORD SEARCH
Circle the words "time."

t	t	i	m	e	e
i	d	u	t	n	
m	x	s	i	c	
e	t	i	m	e	
a	f	t	e	v	

PYRAMID WORDS
-4-
Build a pyramid for the word "time."

1. _____

2. _____ _____

3. _____ _____ _____

4. _____ _____ _____ _____

(The first letter goes on the top line. The first and second letters go on the second line and so on.)

SCRAMBLED WORDS: Unscramble the letters to spell the word "time." -5-

meti iemt eitm mtie

_____ _____ _____ _____

COLORING WORDS: Color all of the sections that have the word "time." -6-

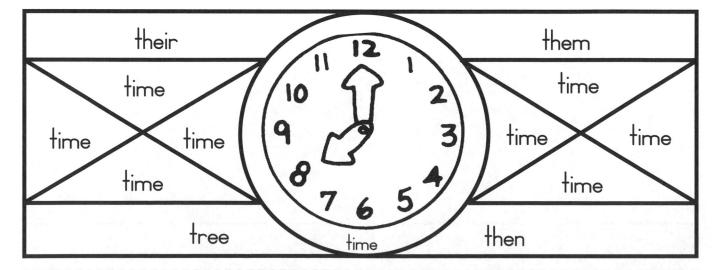

their — time — time — time — time — tree — them — time — time — time — then

See. Say. Rainbow trace.

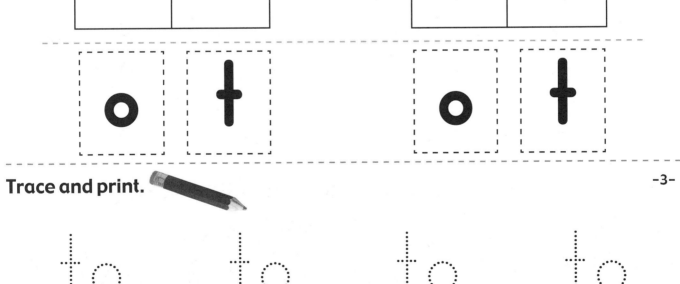

Cut and Paste.

Trace and print.

to   to   to   to

WORD SEARCH
Circle the words "to."

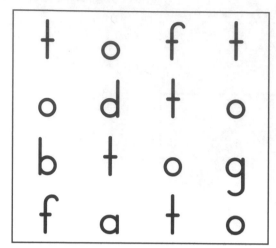

t o f t
o d t o
b t o g
f a t o

PYRAMID WORDS
-4-
Build a pyramid for the word "to."

1. _t_____

2. _____ _____

(The first letter goes on the top line. The first and second letters go on the second line and so on.)

MISSING LETTERS: Fill in the missing letters for the word "to." -5-

COLORING WORDS: Color all of the candies that have the word "to." -6-

See. Say. Rainbow trace.

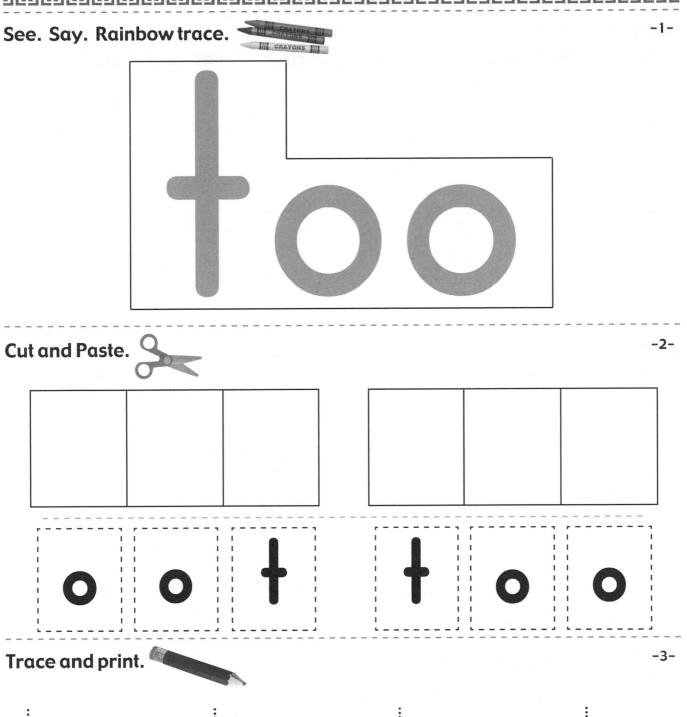

Cut and Paste.

Trace and print.

too   too   too   too

BLEND THE WORD
Draw a line to make the word "too."

TIC-TAC-TOE
Circle the letters that spell "too."

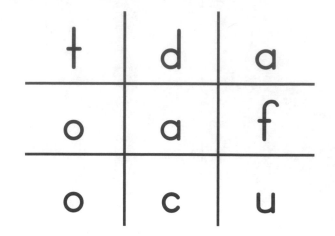

t	d	a
o	a	f
o	c	u

PYRAMID WORDS
Build a pyramid for the word "too."

1. _t_____

2. _____ _____

3. _____ _____ _____

(The first letter goes on the top line. The first and second letters go on the second line and so on.)

DOT-TO-DOT
Connect the letters that spell "too."

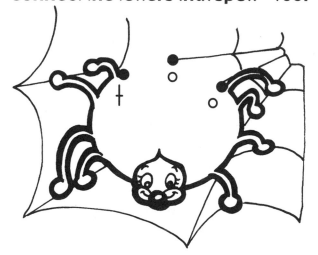

FINISH THE SENTENCE
Use the word "too" to fill in the blanks. Read each sentence.

1. I want to go _____ .

2. I like this _____ .

3. I went with her _____ .

See. Say. Rainbow trace.

Cut and Paste.

e t e r

Trace and print.

tree tree tree tree

_____   _____   _____   _____

WORD TIC-TAC-TOE
Circle the words "tree."

there	tree	three
three	tree	then
their	tree	there

LETTER MAZE
Circle the letters that spell "tree."

MISSING LETTERS: Fill in the missing letters for the word "tree."

t ___ ___ e

t ___ e ___

___ r ___ e

t r ___ ___ ___

SPELL IT! Circle all of the words that spell "tree."

Cut and Paste. -2-

Trace and print. -3-

WORD SEARCH
Circle the words " two."

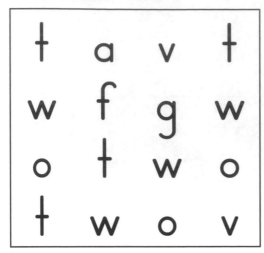

PYRAMID WORDS
Build a pyramid for the word " two."

1. _____

2. _____ _____

3. _____ _____ _____

(The first letter goes on the top line. The first and second letters go on the second line and so on.)

SCRAMBLED WORDS: Unscramble the letters to spell the word " two."

_____   _____   _____

COLORING WORDS!
Color all of the sections that have the word " two."

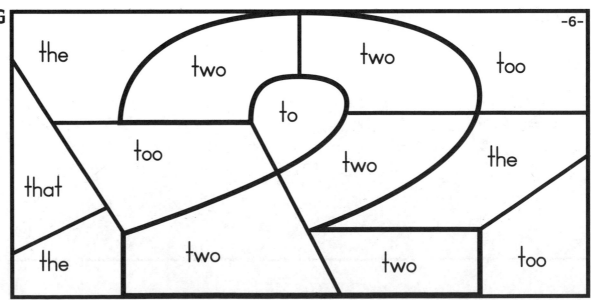

See. Say. Rainbow trace. -1-

Cut and Paste. -2-

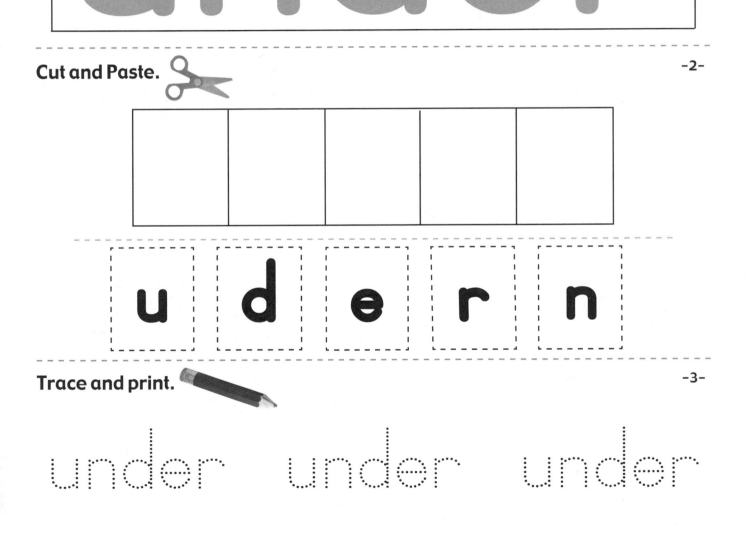

u d e r n

Trace and print. -3-

under   under   under

BLEND THE WORD
Draw a line to make the word "under."

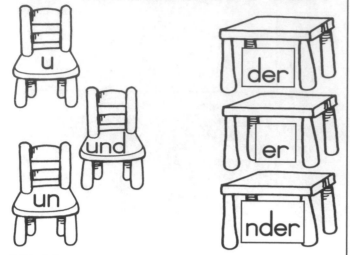

WORD TIC-TAC-TOE
Circle the words "under."

us	water	use
under	under	under
water	use	us

LETTER CONNECT
Connect the letters that spell "under."

DOT-TO-DOT
Connect the letters that spell "under."

FINISH THE SENTENCE
Use the word "under" to fill in the blanks. Read each sentence.

1. The cat is _____ the table.

2. I am _____ the slide.

3. Is the cat _____ the tree?

See. Say. Rainbow trace.

up

Cut and Paste.

p   u   p   u

Trace and print.

up   up   up   up

_____   _____   _____   _____

WORD TIC-TAC-TOE
Circle the words "up."

up	use	is
up	us	use
up	an	us

WORD MAZE
Circle all the words that spell "up."

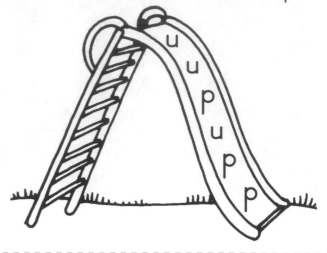

MISSING LETTERS: Fill in the missing letters for the word " up."

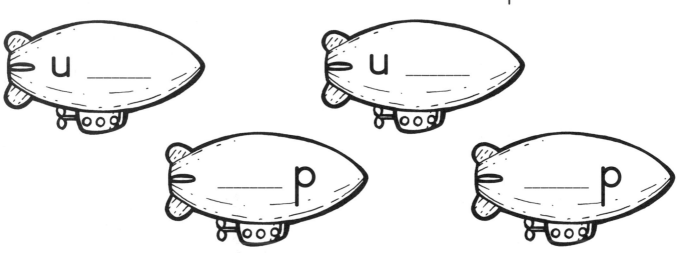

COLORING WORDS: Color all of the birdhouses that have the word " up."

See. Say. Rainbow trace.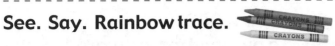

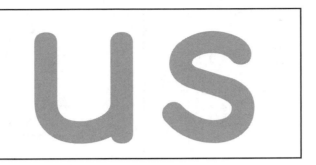

Cut and Paste. ✂

s   u   s   u

Trace and print. ✏

US   US   US   US

_____ _____ _____ _____

WORD SEARCH
Circle the words " us."

u	s	u	s
a	u	s	o
u	n	c	u
s	e	u	s

PYRAMID WORDS
Build a pyramid for the word " us."
–4–

1. _____u_____

2. _____ _____

(The first letter goes on the top line. The first and second letters go on the second line and so on.)

MISSING LETTERS: Fill in the missing letters for the word " us."
–5–

COLORING WORDS: Color all of the bugs that have the word " us."
–6–

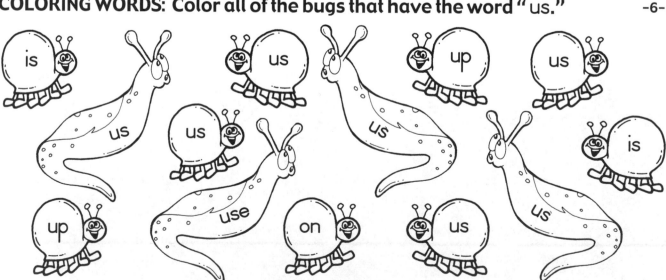

See. Say. Rainbow trace.

Cut and Paste. ✂

| e | s | u | | u | e | s |

Trace and print.

use   use   use   use

_____ _____ _____ _____

BLEND THE WORD
Draw a line to make the word "use."

u

e

us

se

TIC-TAC-TOE
Circle the letters that spell "use."

u	s	e
v	t	o
n	a	f

LETTER CONNECT
Connect the letters that spell "use."

e

u

s

DOT-TO-DOT
Connect the letters that spell "use."

PEANUT
BUTTER

e

u

s

FINISH THE SENTENCE

Use the word "use" to fill in the blanks. Read each sentence.

1. Did you _____ my pencil?

2. May I _____ your paint?

3. I let her _____ my bike.

See. Say. Rainbow trace.

Cut and Paste.

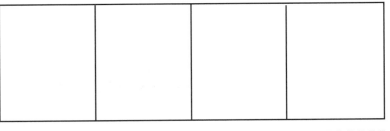

Trace and print.

very   very   very   very

WORD TIC-TAC-TOE
Circle the words "very."

use	every	every
vine	every	use
very	very	very

WORD MAZE
Circle the words "very."

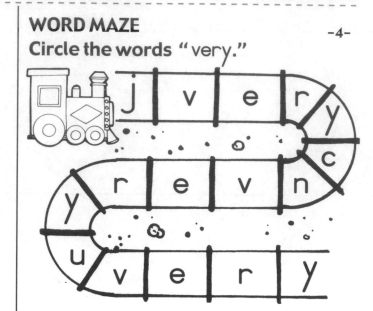

MISSING LETTERS: Fill in the missing letters for the word "very."

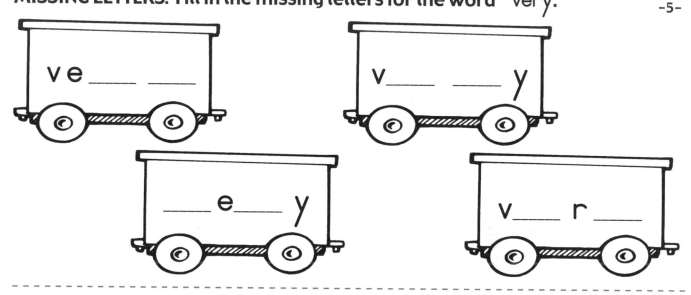

v e ___ ___

v ___ ___ y

___ e ___ y

v ___ r ___

COLORING WORDS: Color all of the train cars that have the word "very."

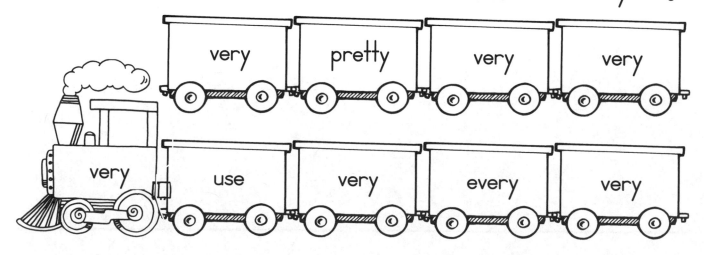

very | pretty | very | very

very | use | very | every | very

walk

a w k l

walk   walk   walk   walk

_____   _____   _____   _____

WORD SEARCH
Circle the words "walk."

z w a l k
w a l k w
a l v m a
l k f d l
k w a l k

PYRAMID WORDS
-4-
Build a pyramid for the word "walk."

1. __w__

2. ____ ____

3. ____ ____ ____

4. ____ ____ ____ ____

(The first letter goes on the top line. The first and second letters go on the second line and so on.)

SCRAMBLED WORDS: Unscramble the letters to spell the word "walk."   -5-

lkaw   lwak   alwk   wkla

_____   _____   _____   _____

COLORING WORDS: Color all of the cars that have the word "walk."   -6-

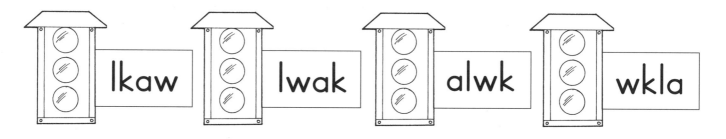

well   walk   water   walk   went

walk   walk   want   walk   walk

See. Say. Rainbow trace. —1—

Cut and Paste. ✂ —2—

n   w   t   a

Trace and print. ✏ —3—

want   want   want   want

_____   _____   _____   _____

BLEND THE WORD
Draw a line to make the word "want."

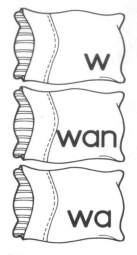

WORD TIC-TAC-TOE
Circle the words "want."

want	well	what
want	what	went
want	went	water

LETTER CONNECT
Connect the letters that spell "want."

DOT-TO-DOT
Connect the letters that spell "want."

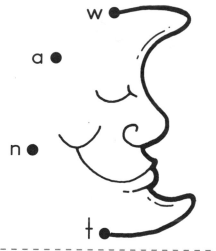

FINISH THE SENTENCE
Use the word "want" to fill in the blanks. Read each sentence.

1. I _____ to go with you.

2. I _____ a new dog.

3. Do you _____ to play with me?

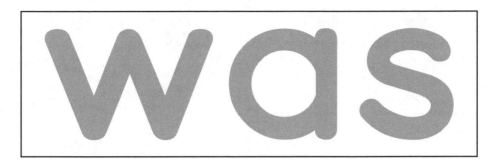

was

Cut and Paste. -2-

a w s   s a w

Trace and print. -3-

was   was   was   was

_____   _____   _____   _____

TIC-TAC-TOE
Circle the letters that spell " was."

v	w	m
o	a	i
c	s	u

LETTER MAZE
Circle the letters that spell " was."

MISSING LETTERS: Fill in the missing letters for the word " was."

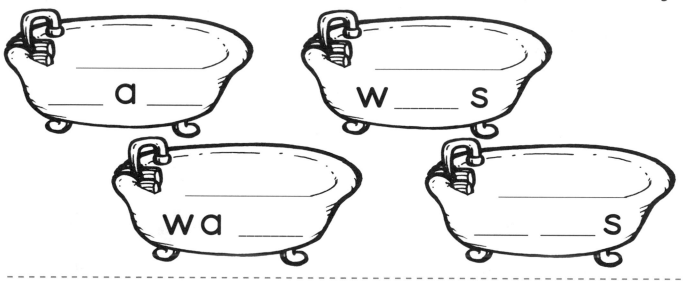

_____ a _____

w _____ s

wa _____

_____ s

COLORING WORDS:
Color all of the ducks that have the word " was."

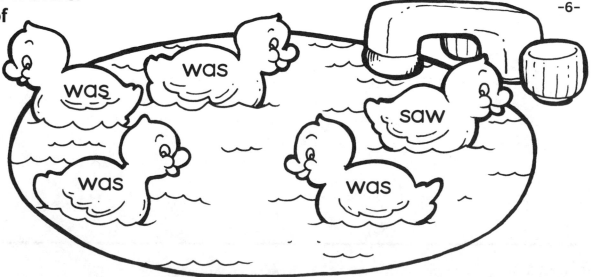

See. Say. Rainbow trace.

water

Cut and Paste. ✂

t   a   e   w   r

Trace and print.

water   water   water

_____   _____   _____

WORD SEARCH
Circle the words "water."

w	w	a	t	e	r
w	a	t	e	r	w
v	t	t	z	l	a
z	e	f	e	d	t
c	r	m	u	r	e
d	w	a	t	e	r

PYRAMID WORDS
Build a pyramid for the word "water."   -4-

1. __w__
2. ____ ____
3. ____ ____ ____
4. ____ ____ ____ ____
5. ____ ____ ____ ____ ____

(The first letter goes on the top line. The first and second letters go on the second line and so on.)

SCRAMBLED WORDS: Unscramble the letters to spell the word "water."   -5-

tewra   eatwr   erwta   atewr

____ ____ ____ ____

COLORING WORDS: Color all of the petals that have the word "water."   -6-

See. Say. Rainbow trace.

Cut and Paste. ✂

e w   e w

Trace and print.

we   we   we   we

_____   _____   _____   _____

PYRAMID WORDS
Build a pyramid for the word " we."

1. ___W___

2. _____ _____

(The first letter goes on the top line. The first and second letters go on the second line and so on.)

we	will	was
was	we	will
went	was	we

MISSING LETTERS
Fill in the missing letters for the word " we."

FINISH THE SENTENCE
-6-
Use the word " we" to fill in the blanks. Read each sentence.

1. Where should _____ go?

2. _____ are going to have fun!

3. _____ will ride our bikes.

See. Say. Rainbow trace.

Cut and Paste.

l w l e

Trace and print.

well   well   well   well

WORD TIC–TAC–TOE
Circle the words "well."

we	went	well
went	was	well
was	we	well

LETTER MAZE
-4-

Circle the letters that spell "well."

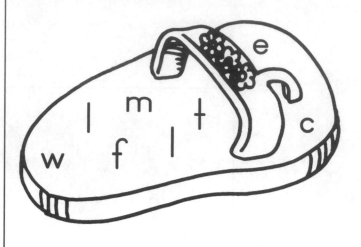

MISSING LETTERS: Fill in the missing letters for the word "well."
-5-

COLORING WORDS: Color all of the pails that have the word "well."
-6-

See. Say. Rainbow trace.

Cut and Paste.

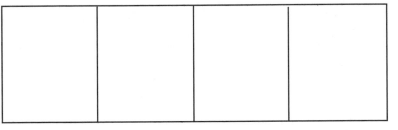

Trace and print.

WORD SEARCH
Circle the words "went."

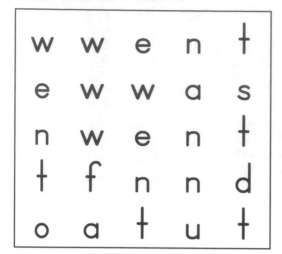

w	w	e	n	t
e	w	w	a	s
n	w	e	n	t
t	f	n	n	d
o	a	t	u	t

PYRAMID WORDS
Build a pyramid for the word "went." -4-

1. ___w___

2. ___ ___

3. ___ ___ ___

4. ___ ___ ___ ___

(The first letter goes on the top line. The first and second letters go on the second line and so on.)

SCRAMBLED WORDS: Unscramble the letters to spell the word "went." -5-

ntwe   wetn   etwn   tenw

_____   _____   _____   _____

SPELL IT! Circle all of the words that spell "went." -6-

went / want

white / went

went / was

went / when

where / went

were / went

went / who

See. Say. Rainbow trace.

Cut and Paste.

e e w e r

Trace and print.

were   were   were

_____   _____   _____

BLEND THE WORD
Draw a line to make the word " were."

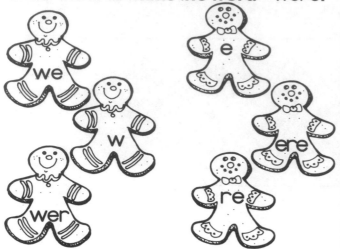

WORD TIC-TAC-TOE
-4-
Circle the words " were."

were	we	went
were	went	where
were	where	we

LETTER CONNECT
Connect the letters that spell " were."

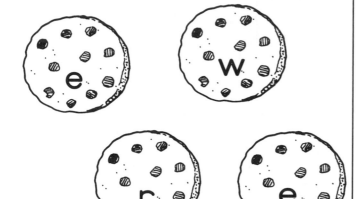

DOT-TO-DOT
-5-
Connect the letters that spell " were."

FINISH THE SENTENCE
-6-
Use the word " were" to fill in the blanks. Read each sentence.

1. Where _____ the kids going?

2. We _____ at the zoo.

3. _____ they going to come with us?

See. Say. Rainbow trace.

what

Cut and Paste.

h　　w　　t　　a

Trace and print.

what what what what

_____　_____　_____　_____

WORD TIC-TAC-TOE
Circle the words "what."

want	was	where
what	what	what
was	went	want

LETTER MAZE
-4-
Circle the letters that spell "what."

MISSING LETTERS: Fill in the missing letters for the word "what."
-5-

w h ___ ___

w ___ a ___

___ h ___ t

w ___ ___ t

SPELL IT! Circle all of the words that spell "what."
-6-

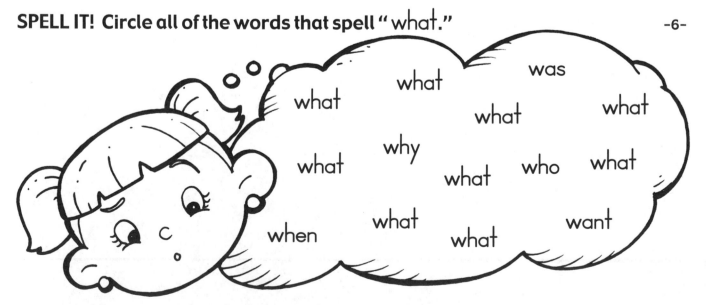

what   was
what   what
            what
why
what   what   what
        what   who
what   want
when   what

See. Say. Rainbow trace.

when

Cut and Paste.

h   w   n   e

Trace and print.

when when when when

_____   _____   _____   _____

WORD SEARCH
Circle the words "when."

w	w	h	e	n
h	w	w	c	v
e	w	h	e	n
n	b	e	e	u
z	f	n	d	n

PYRAMID WORDS
-4-

Build a pyramid for the word "when."

1. __w__

2. ____ ____

3. ____ ____ ____

4. ____ ____ ____ ____

(The first letter goes on the top line. The first and second letters go on the second line and so on.)

SCRAMBLED WORDS: Unscramble the letters to spell the word "when." -5-

_____ _____ _____ _____

COLORING WORDS: Color all of the flags that have the word "when." -6-

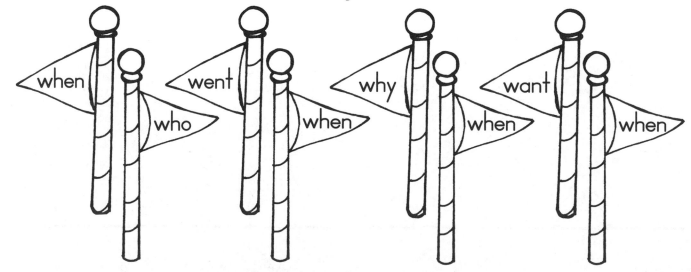

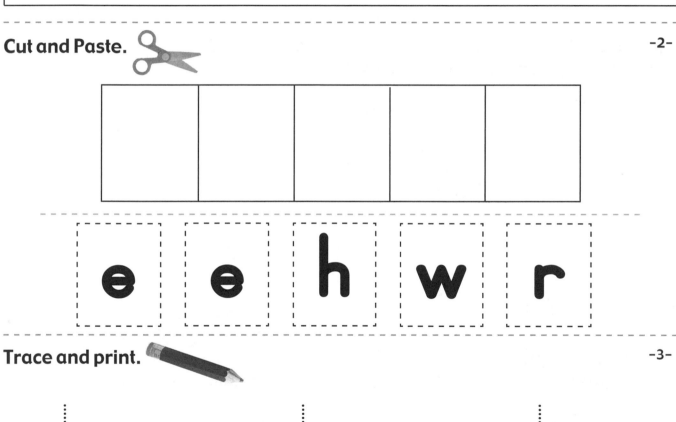

Cut and Paste. -2-

e   e   h   w   r

Trace and print. -3-

where   where   where

BLEND THE WORD
Draw a line to make the word "where."

whe

w

wh

wher

here

e

re

ere

WORD TIC-TAC-TOE
Circle the words "where."

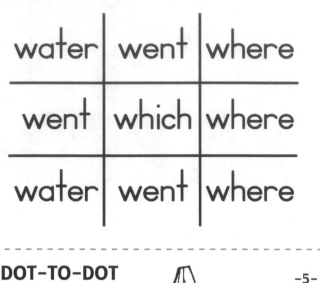

water	went	where
went	which	where
water	went	where

LETTER CONNECT
Connect the letters that spell "where."

e

r

w

e

h

DOT-TO-DOT
Connect the letters that spell "where."

FINISH THE SENTENCE
Use the word "where" to fill in the blanks. Read each sentence.

1. _____ are we going?

2. This is _____ I want to play.

3. _____ is your friend?

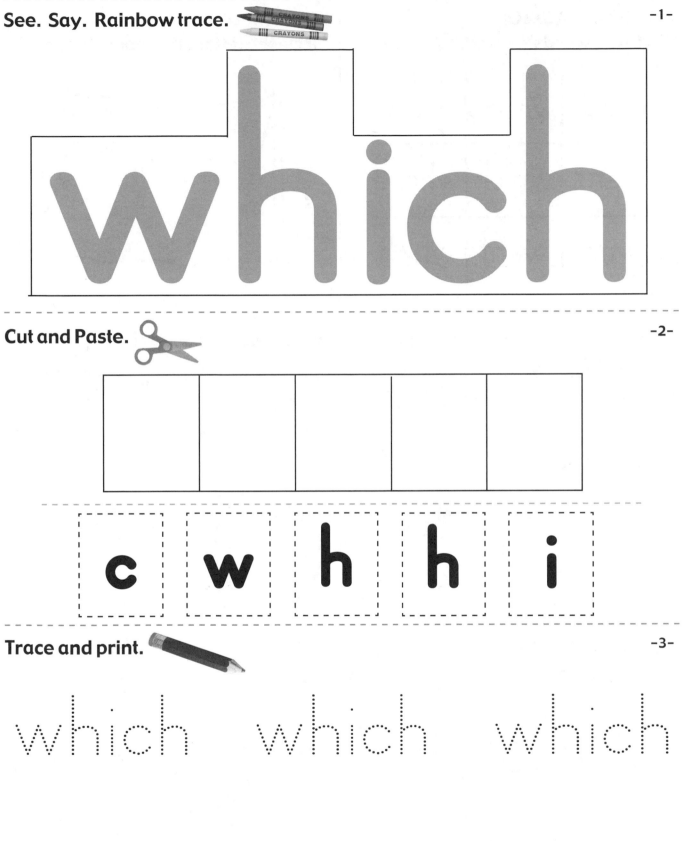

Cut and Paste. -2-

Trace and print. -3-

which   which   which

WORD TIC-TAC-TOE
Circle the words "which."

which	where	with
went	which	where
with	went	which

LETTER MAZE
Circle the letters that spell "which."

MISSING LETTERS: Fill in the missing letters for the word "which."

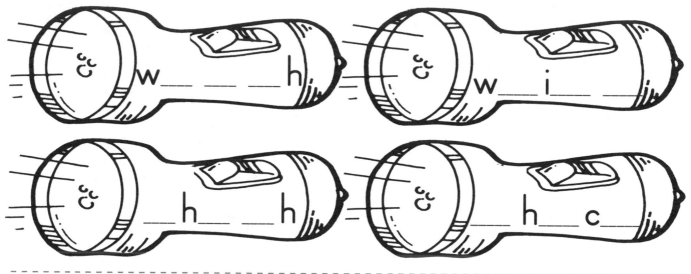

w __ __ __ h

w __ __ __ i

__ h __ __ h

__ __ h __ c

COLORING WORDS: Color all of the tents that have the word "which."

See. Say. Rainbow trace.

white

Cut and Paste.

e   w   i   t   h

Trace and print.

white   white   white

_____   _____   _____

WORD SEARCH
Circle the words "white."

w	h	i	t	e	w
w	n	z	d	w	h
h	a	c	r	h	i
i	q	p	e	i	t
t	w	h	i	t	e
e	d	n	x	e	v

PYRAMID WORDS
-4-
Build a pyramid for the word "white."

1. __W__

2. ___ ___

3. ___ ___ ___

4. ___ ___ ___ ___

5. ___ ___ ___ ___ ___

(The first letter goes on the top line. The first and second letters go on the second line and so on.)

SCRAMBLED WORDS: Unscramble the letters to spell the word "white." -5-

ewith   tehwi   htiew   thiwe

_____   _____

COLORING WORDS: Color all of the rabbit ears that have the word "white." -6-

See. Say. Rainbow trace.

who

Cut and Paste.

o	w	h

h	o	w

Trace and print.

who   who   who   who

_____ _____ _____ _____

BLEND THE WORD
Draw a line to make the word "who."

w

o

wh

ho

Circle the letters that spell "who."

c	t	c
w	h	o
u	m	q

LETTER CONNECT
Connect the letters that spell "who."

w

h

o

Connect the letters that spell "who."

w

h

o

Use the word "who" to fill in the blanks. Read each sentence.

1. _____ was at the door?

2. _____ did their homework?

3. _____ was on the phone?

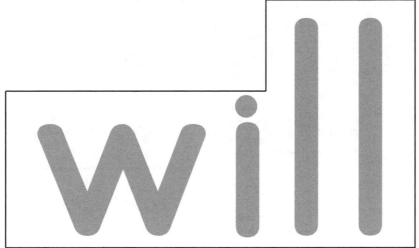

Cut and Paste. -2-

l   w   l   i

Trace and print. -3-

will   will   will   will

———   ———   ———   ———

BLEND THE WORD
Draw a line to make the word "will."

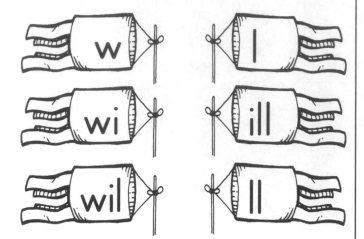

WORD TIC-TAC-TOE
Circle the words "will."

will	with	who
who	will	white
with	with	will

LETTER CONNECT
Connect the letters that spell "will."

DOT-TO-DOT
Connect the letters that spell "will."

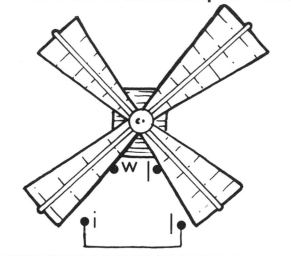

FINISH THE SENTENCE
Use the word "will" to fill in the blanks. Read each sentence.

1. Where _____ you go today?

2. _____ your mom make cookies?

3. What _____ your dog eat?

See. Say. Rainbow trace.

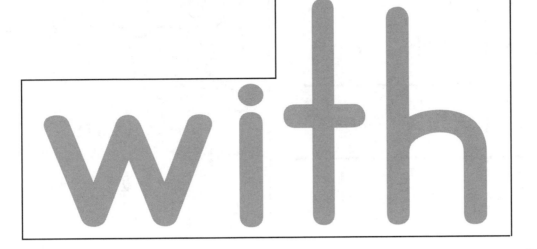

Cut and Paste.

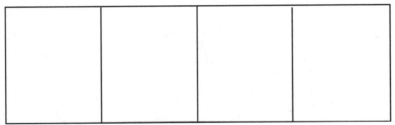

| h | w | t | i |

Trace and print.

with   with   with

WORD TIC-TAC-TOE
Circle the words "with."

with	with	with
which	white	went
white	want	who

LETTER MAZE
Circle the letters that spell "with."

-4-

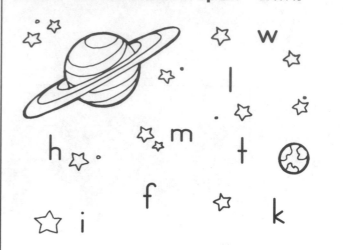

w
l
m
t
h
f
k
i

MISSING LETTERS: Fill in the missing letters for the word "with."
-5-

w__t__   w____h   __i__h

SPELL IT! Circle all of the words that spell "with."
-6-

why   with   with

who   was   with

with   with   with   went

See. Say. Rainbow trace.

Cut and Paste.

r   w   k   o

Trace and print.

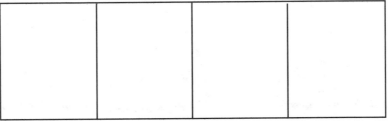

work work work work

_____   _____   _____   _____

WORD TIC-TAC-TOE
Circle the words " work."

work	what	who
work	who	white
work	want	want

LETTER MAZE

Circle the letters that spell " work."

-4-

k m
c h o
w
n
r

MISSING LETTERS: Fill in the missing letters for the word " work."

-5-

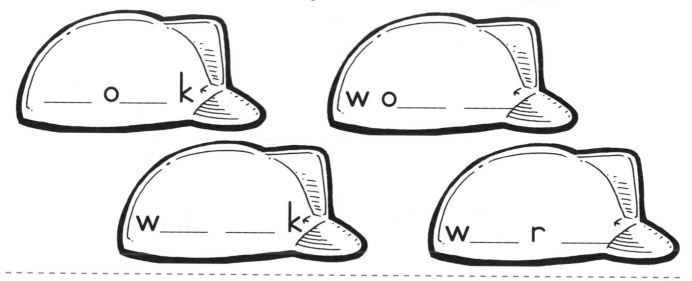

___ o ___ k

w o ___ ___

w ___ ___ k

w ___ r ___

COLORING WORDS: Color all of the windows that have the word " work."

-6-

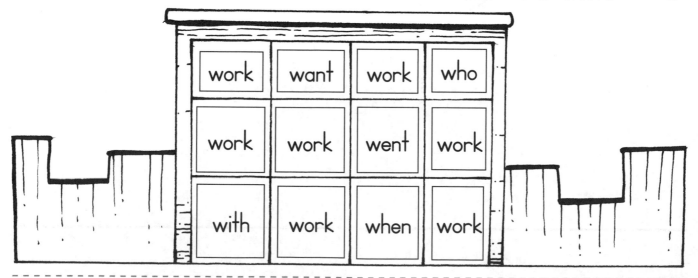

work	want	work	who
work	work	went	work
with	work	when	work

See. Say. Rainbow trace.

Cut and Paste. ✂ -2-

d   w   l   o   u

Trace and print. -3-

would   would   would

WORD SEARCH
Circle the words "would."

w	w	m	z	v	w
w	o	u	l	d	o
d	u	u	h	j	u
s	l	n	l	t	l
a	d	p	v	d	d
w	o	u	l	d	t

PYRAMID WORDS
Build a pyramid for the word "would." -4-

1. __w__
2. ____ ____
3. ____ ____ ____
4. ____ ____ ____ ____
5. ____ ____ ____ ____ ____

(The first letter goes on the top line. The first and second letters go on the second line and so on.)

SCRAMBLED WORDS: Unscramble the letters to spell the word "would." -5-

louwd   wduol   wludo   ldwuo

_____   _____   _____   _____

COLORING WORDS: Color all of the apples that have the word "would." -6-

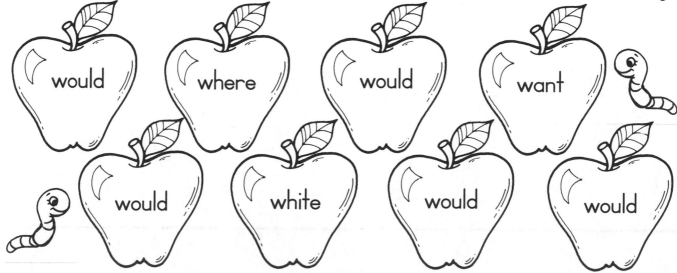

would   where   would   want

would   white   would   would

yellow

Cut and Paste.

e l o y l w

Trace and print.

yellow   yellow   yellow

_____   _____   _____

WORD SEARCH
Circle the words "yellow."

y	y	p	o	f	y
e	e	a	c	v	e
l	l	l	m	q	l
l	l	z	l	u	l
o	o	k	n	o	o
w	w	d	f	r	w

PYRAMID WORDS
-4-
Build a pyramid for the word "yellow."

1. _y_
2. ____ ____
3. ____ ____ ____
4. ____ ____ ____ ____
5. ____ ____ ____ ____ ____
6. ____ ____ ____ ____ ____ ____

(The first letter goes on the top line. The first and second letters go on the second line and so on.)

SCRAMBLED WORDS: Unscramble the letters to spell the word "yellow." -5-

_____ _____ _____ _____

COLORING WORDS: Color all of the lemons that have the word "yellow." -6-

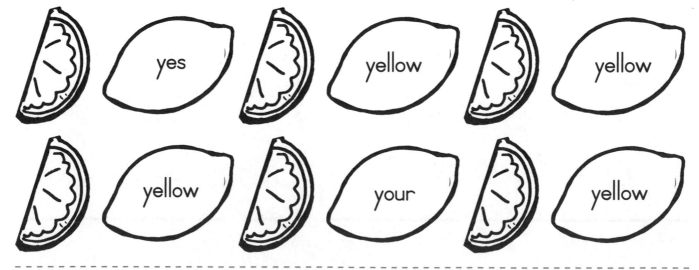

See. Say. Rainbow trace.

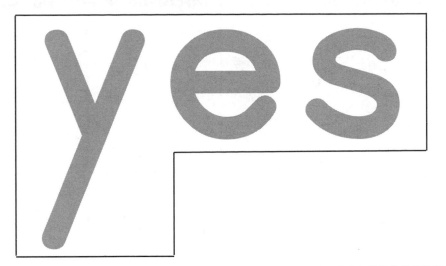

Cut and Paste.

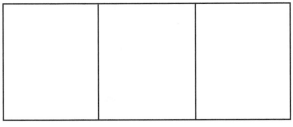

Trace and print.

yes   yes   yes   yes

_____   _____   _____   _____

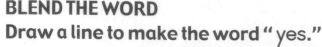

BLEND THE WORD
Draw a line to make the word "yes."

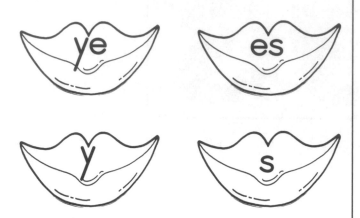

TIC-TAC-TOE
-4-
Circle the letters that spell "yes."

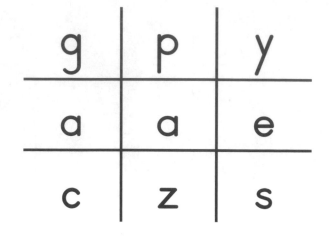

PYRAMID WORDS
Build a pyramid for the word "yes."

1. ___y___

2. _____ _____

3. _____ _____ _____

(The first letter goes on the top line. The first and second letters go on the second line and so on.)

DOT-TO-DOT
-5-
Connect the letters that spell "yes."

FINISH THE SENTENCE
-6-
Use the word "yes" to fill in the blanks. Read each sentence.

1. _____, I would like to go.

2. I said, "_____, I like it."

3. My mom said, "_____, I can play."

KE-804038 © Key Education -354- *The Best Sight Word Book Ever!*

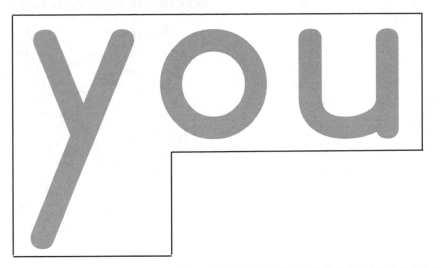

Cut and Paste. −2−

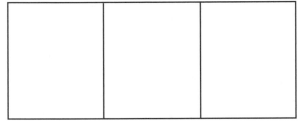

Trace and print. −3−

you   you   you   you

_____   _____   _____   _____

TIC–TAC–TOE
Circle the letters that spell " you."

p	e	z
s	a	n
y	o	u

LETTER MAZE
Circle the letters that spell " you."

MISSING LETTERS: Fill in the missing letters for the word " you."

COLORING WORDS: Color all of the rockets that have the word " you."

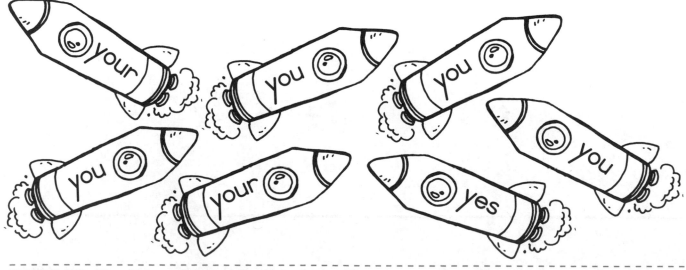

See. Say. Rainbow trace.

Cut and Paste.

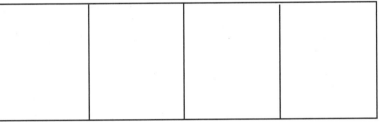

Trace and print.

your   your   your

WORD SEARCH
Circle the words "your."

y	o	u	r	y
v	o	c	n	o
n	z	u	a	u
y	o	u	r	r
a	y	o	u	r

PYRAMID WORDS   –4–
Build a pyramid for the word "your."

1. ___y___

2. _____ _____

3. _____ _____ _____

4. _____ _____ _____ _____

(The first letter goes on the top line. The first and second letters go on the second line and so on.)

SCRAMBLED WORDS: Unscramble the letters to spell the word "your." –5–

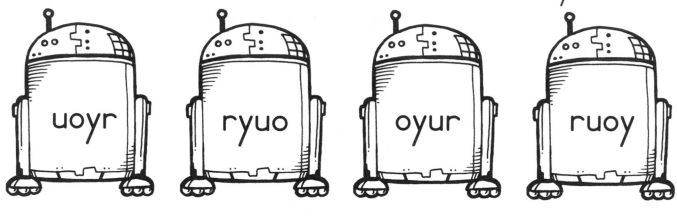

uoyr   ryuo   oyur   ruoy

_____ _____ _____ _____

SPELL IT! Circle all of the words that spell "your." –6–

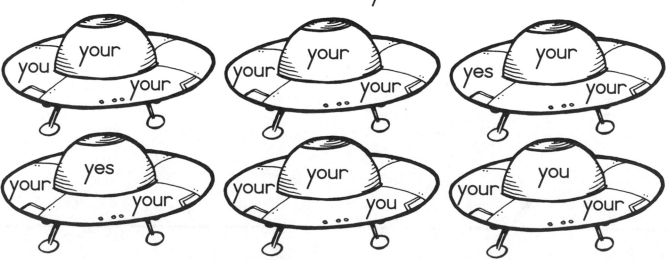

Reproducible Words for the Classroom Word Wall

a

about

after

all

again

am

an

and

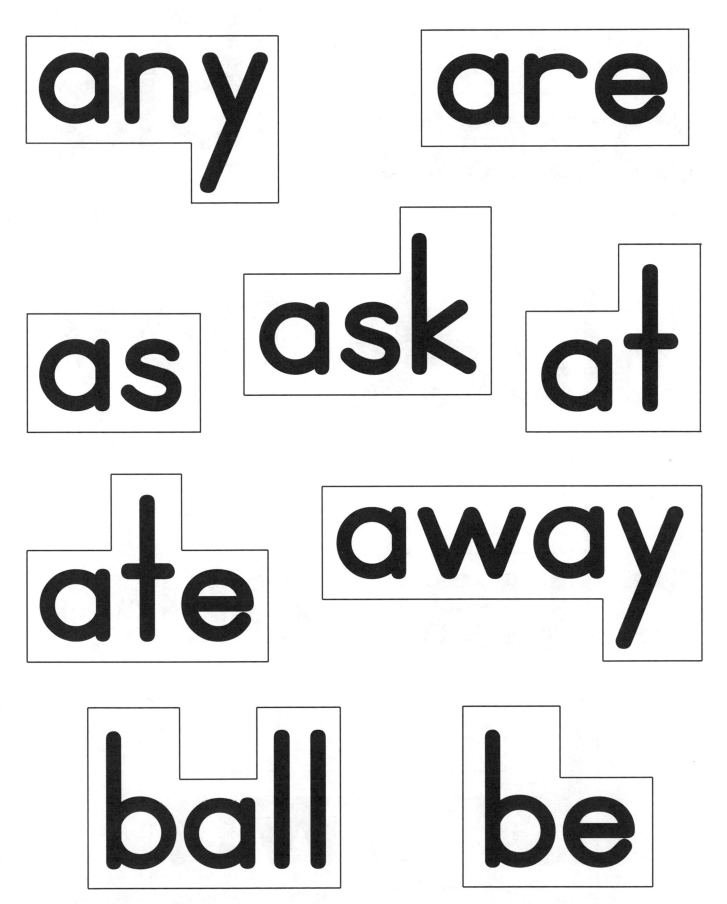

any

are

as

ask

at

ate

away

ball

be

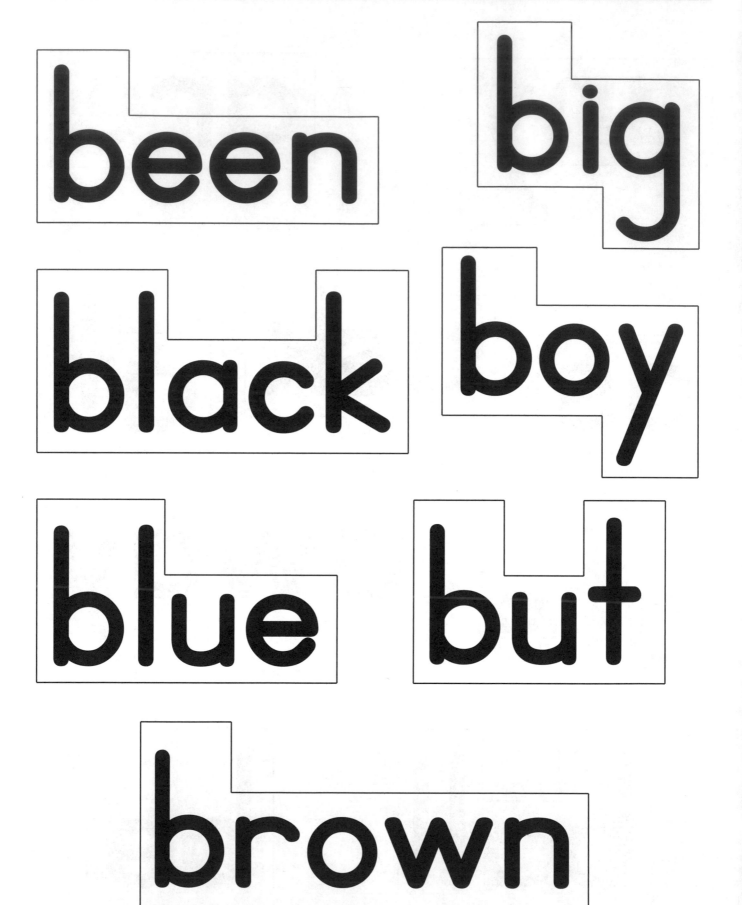

been

big

black

boy

blue

but

brown

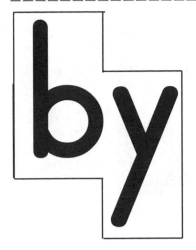

by

came

call

can

come

cat

could dad

day

did

do

down

dog

each

eat

eight

every fly

find first

five four

for from

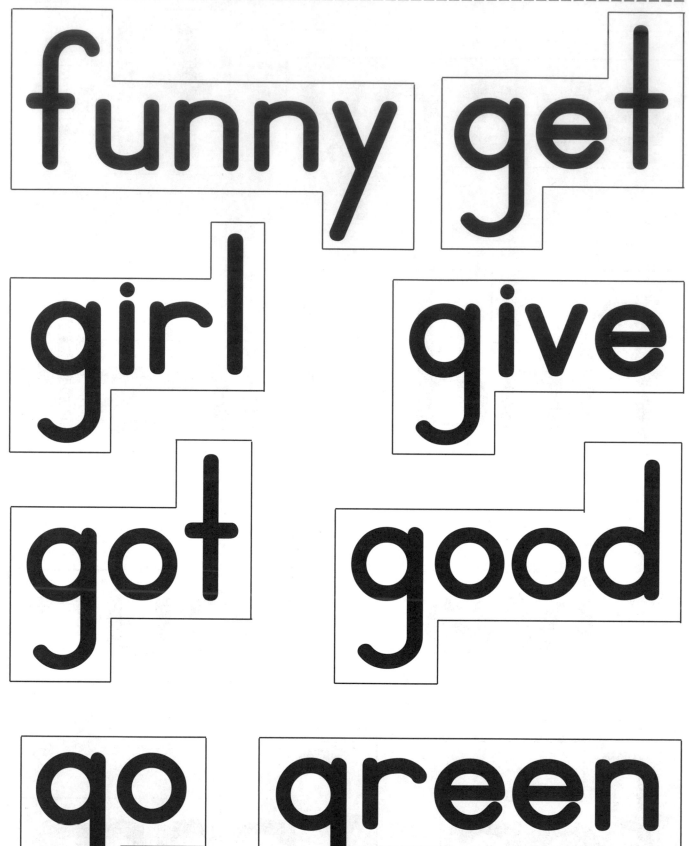

funny get

girl give

got good

go green

had

has

have

he

help

her

here

him

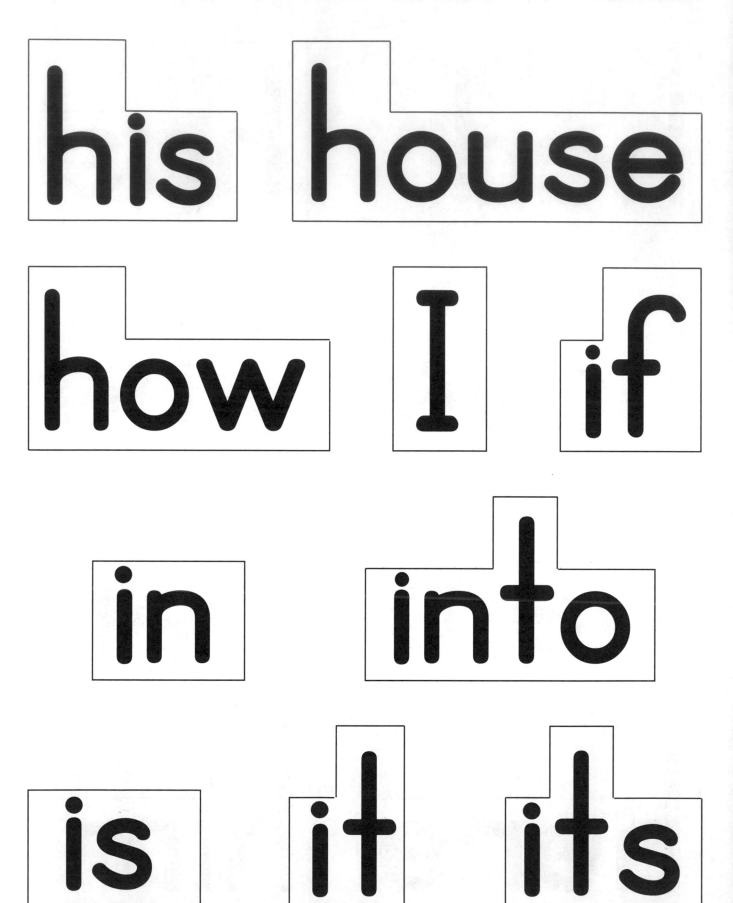

his house

how I if

in into

is it its

jump let

just long

little look

like made

mom may

me many

new

my

must

make

nine

no

not

now

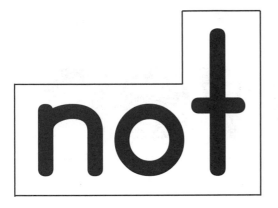

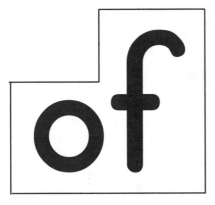

on

one

or

orange

our

over

people

out

play

please

pretty

purple

put

ran

-373-

red ride

run said

saw say

school

see seven

she six

so some

soon stop

take than

ten their

that the

thank

time this

three too

two tree

to under

up

very

use

walk

was

want

us

water

-379-

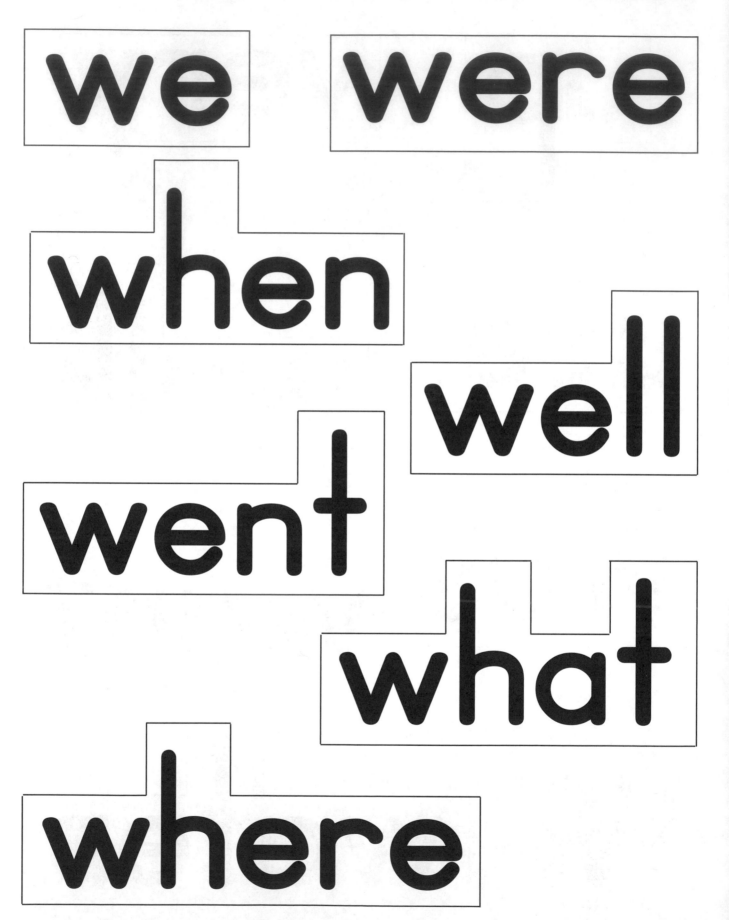

we

were

when

well

went

what

where

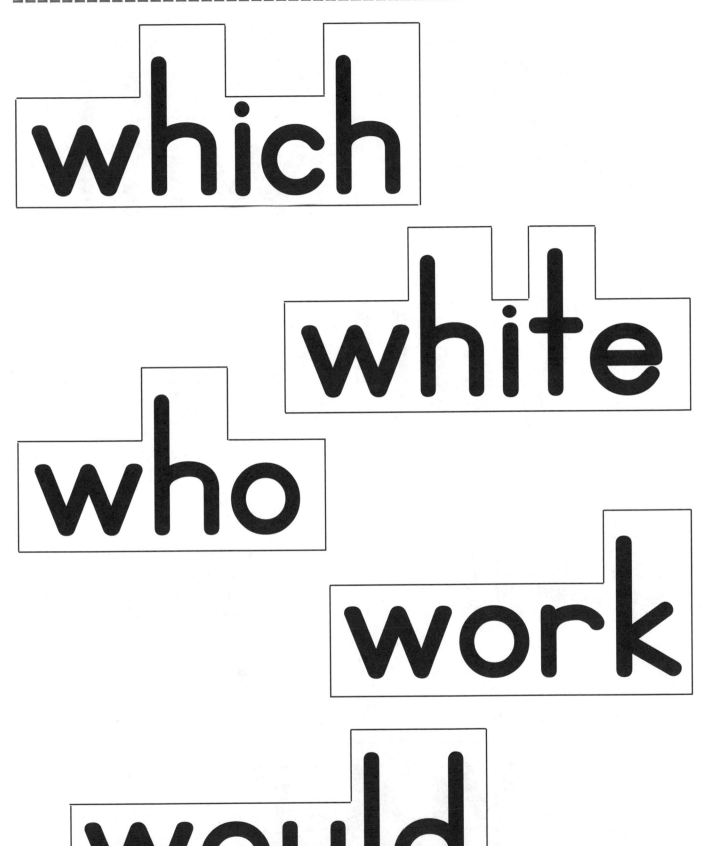

which

white

who

work

would

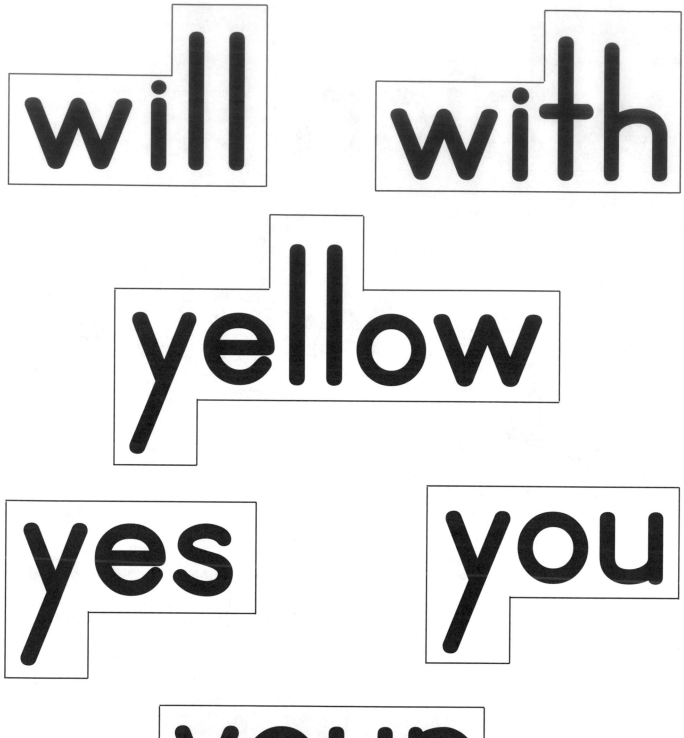

will

with

yellow

yes

you

your

The Best Sight Word Book Ever! supports the NCTE/IRA *Standards for the English Language Arts* and the recommended teaching practices outlined in the NAEYC/IRA position statement *"Learning to Read and Write: Developmentally Appropriate Practices for Young Children."*

Each activity in this book supports one or more of the following standards:

1. **Students read many different types of print and nonprint texts for a variety of purposes.**
    Students read a wide variety of sight words and sentences while doing the activities in this book.

2. **Students use a variety of strategies to build meaning while reading.**
    The activities in this book promote sight word recognition, an essential skill in learning to read.

3. **Students communicate in spoken, written, and visual form for a variety of purposes and a variety of audiences.**
    In this book students write sight words, do chants and songs, and create art projects to support their learning of sight words and to show what they have learned.

4. **Students become participating members in a variety of literacy communities.**
    The Best Sight Word Book Ever! contains many group activities, helping teachers build a literacy community in their classroom.

NAEYC/IRA Position Statement *Learning to Read and Write: Developmentally Appropriate Practices for Young Children*

Each activity in this book supports one or more of the following recommended teaching practices for Kindergarten and Primary students:

1. **Teachers read to children daily and provide opportunities for students to independently read both fiction and nonfiction texts.**
    In *The Best Sight Word Book Ever!,* students read words and sentences in order to learn sight words.

2. **Teachers provide balanced literacy instruction that incorporates systematic phonics instruction along with meaningful reading and writing activities.**
    The Best Sight Word Book Ever! supports the learning of sight words by incorporating them into a variety of reading activities.

3. **Teachers provide opportunities for students to write many different kinds of text for different purposes.**
    Students learn to write a variety of sight words through the activities in this book.

4. **Teachers provide opportunities for children to work in small groups.**
    The Best Sight Word Book Ever! includes small group activities that help students learn sight words.

5. **Teachers provide challenging instruction that expands children's knowledge of their world and expands vocabulary.**
    The Best Sight Word Book Ever! helps expand children's vocabularies by introducing 170 sight words.

6. **Teachers adapt teaching strategies based on the individual needs of a child.**
    The Best Sight Word Book Ever! incorporates auditory, visual, tactile, and kinesthetic activities so teachers can support different student learning styles.